embrace
your space

embrace
your space

Organizing Ideas and Stylish Upgrades
for Every Room on Any Budget

KATIE HOLDEFEHR

PHOTOGRAPHY BY GENEVIEVE GARRUPPO

weldon**owen**

CONTENTS

INTRODUCTION

We all deserve a home we love—even if we don't plan to stay there forever. Maybe you're renting. Maybe you're in a small home you know your family will one day outgrow. Or maybe you've found a house with good bones to turn into your dream home, but you need affordable decor ideas to tide you over until the grand remodel. For all these situations and more, *Embrace Your Space* will help you make the most of your home—and your life—right now.

Home, even if temporary, can help us feel grounded. At its best, home is a place where we seek comfort and safety, where we let go of the day and recharge for the next, where we connect with those who we love most. Even better if it matches our style, embodies our values, and nurtures our interests. It's a big ask. And it's almost impossible to achieve if we always have one foot out the door. Yet we're continuously bombarded with messaging that dissuades us from investing in our current home until we've "made it." During my time as an editor at *Real Simple*, and previously at *Apartment Therapy*, I noticed a trend: Whenever a beautiful home tour happens to be a rental, readers often ask, "Why do all that for a place you just rent?" Considering that more than forty-three million US households rent their homes (that's more than one-third of all households), according to 2020 data from the US Census Bureau, I don't believe that many people should be denied the joy of a home that reflects them and fits their life.

Of course, this doesn't mean you should spend so much money decorating a rental that you don't save for a down payment if owning a home is your goal. Nor should you splurge so much on temporary upgrades that you can no longer afford the renovation you had planned. But if you're interested in creating a home that supports and improves your life, *Embrace Your Space* will offer ways to do just that on a wide range of budgets. In truth, some of the most transformative ideas within these pages call for a $30 can of paint and a couple of hours of your time. If you knew you were just $30 and 120 minutes away from a home you'd love a little more, why wouldn't you?

Frequently, I find that the hesitation to decorate a "for now" home, regardless of whether it's rented or owned, is partially about the money and partially about the time but mostly a reluctance to invest in where we are. We're hesitant to put our hearts into something that might not last forever. But here's the thing: Your life isn't something that starts when you finally buy a house or can afford a bigger place or stop living with roommates—it's that thing happening right now. You can still work toward your future while honoring your present. This book will help you embrace the home, as well as the phase of life, you're in at this moment.

The six chapters in this book will guide you through the process of embracing your space. You'll organize and decorate your way to a home you love, no matter your budget or how long you plan to stay. We'll begin by identifying your priorities for both your home and your life—they should ideally be linked. They will light the way as you (1) let go of what you don't need; (2) organize, store, and make space for what's most important to you; (3) maximize the square footage you have (no matter whether you're in a 350-square-foot studio or a five-bedroom house); (4) share space and balance priorities with your partner, kids, roommates, or pets; and make your home come alive with (5) houseplants and (6) a dose of color.

As we flow through these six themes, let the twelve home tours inspire you. All measuring less than 1,150 square feet, they make space for everything from home businesses and a family of four to pets, big parties, big personalities, an urban jungle, cherished collections, and countless memories. These homes and the people who live in them are proof that there is no one-size-fits-all approach to our homes or our lives. Peek inside tiny rental apartments in the big city; an RV in the desert providing a tranquil, albeit transient, home for a young family working on a house; an architect-designed loft one family may soon outgrow; and a Memphis home full of stylish stopgaps with a homeowner saving up for a remodel. They will inspire you to DIY a faux marble countertop, try a new organization method, install some peel-and-stick wallpaper, plant a container garden, pick up a paintbrush, and create a home that makes you happy.

All twelve spaces contain brilliant organizing and decor ideas you'll want to borrow, but beyond that, they are case studies on how to craft a deeply personal home, full of stories and soul. They represent a range of styles because each one is a reflection of the people who live there. Yet none of them—from the cabin in the Hollywood Hills to the one-bedroom in Brooklyn—are intended to be forever homes. In keeping with this, several of the people highlighted within these pages have already moved out of the homes featured here—they've gone on to new neighborhoods, new cities, new states, new adventures, and their former homes are now occupied by new couples, new families, new pets, new stories, and (with any luck) fresh layouts and furnishings to suit them. Whether renters or homeowners, we are all stewards of the spaces we inhabit; they tend to outlive us. The best we can do is tailor them to our lives as we wish to live them now.

Chapter 1
MINIMAL

wanderers' rest

KELLY BROWN AND BRYCE EHRECKE

- Yucca Valley, California
- 250 Square Feet
- Owned

Kelly Brown and Bryce Ehrecke met on Christmas Day 2011 in Slab City, an off-the-grid (no electricity, no running water) community built on an abandoned military base in the California desert, a couple of hours south of Joshua Tree. At the time, Bryce was traveling in a 1983 GMC Vandura pop-top camper van—orange exterior, purple crushed velvet interior—along with five friends: Three shared the bed that stretched across the back when the bench seats unfolded, two slept in the bed up top, and one reclined in the passenger seat. He noticed Kelly the second she drove in. There on a solo camping trip and photography assignment, Kelly (who is now a sought-after wedding photographer for those chasing natural light and an ethereal glow) strolled up to where Bryce and friends were playing music and asked to snap his portrait. The camera flashed—immortalizing Bryce with headband-bedecked hair and a knit sweater, cradling a puppy, a glimpse of orange van in the background—and something sparked. "I camped with him and his friends that night, and we've been together ever since," Kelly says.

embrace your space

They spent the next year roaming—first by van, later in a station wagon that Bryce converted to run on vegetable oil—around California, then down to Mexico to work on a natural building project (Bryce is the founder of Cré Natural Building), where they got engaged just three months after meeting. They headed back to California, on to Ohio to see Kelly's family, up to British Columbia to visit Bryce's family, before swinging back down to California for their intimate wedding at a friend's farm in Ojai. By 2018, the couple had settled down just slightly, spending summers in Victoria on Vancouver Island and winters in Joshua Tree, a cadence that let Kelly follow the wedding season in each locale. Needing to establish a desert home base quickly, their shared history made the decision easy: They would refurbish a trailer. One visit to the RV Depot later, they bought a mid-century Spartan Royal Mansion, complete with warm wood paneling and a kitchen in cringeworthy-yet-functional condition, for $11,000.

BELOW: *By downsizing to the trailer, the couple has reclaimed time previously spent on cleaning. "It takes five minutes to tidy it, and five minutes if you want to wash the floors or wipe the counters down," Bryce says. "And I feel like it doesn't really get messy, either, because everything that's in there has a spot to go," Kelly adds.*

To minimize the environmental impact of the remodel, they salvaged as much of the existing interior as possible and sourced local supplies. The kitchen cabinets and floors were painted white, while the hardware got a dose of bronze spray paint. Rather than rip out the dated backsplash, they refreshed it with a coat of paint mixed with sand from the wash, a nearby streambed that only flows with water following heavy rains. The new bar counter and L-shaped bench seating were constructed from western maple, a material that didn't have to travel too far. The trailer was move-in ready within six weeks.

The RV's aluminum exterior stands in stark metallic contrast to its sandy surroundings, but inside, the color palette—burnt orange, dusty beige—reflects the landscape outside.

"I always really loved the desert," Kelly says. "It's a very different environment than I grew up in, but it's always been a place that feels very calming and relaxing. And visually, I just love the vastness and the monochromatic colors." The trailer may measure only 8 feet wide by 31 feet long, yet Kelly embraced a style with "lots of room to breathe and lots of visual breaks." Taking cues from the desert, she sought a space free from both the physical clutter of excess belongings and the visual clutter of "too much color or pattern or texture." The minimalist design helps her focus, as she spends hours at a computer editing photos when she's not driving around to weddings.

To keep surfaces clear, all the storage is hidden away. The bed lifts up to stash a suitcase; a separate drawer under the bed stores sheets; the closet holds the couple's coats, hanging clothes, and shoes for all seasons; even more storage lies below the bench seating. "That's the nice thing about the trailer, too; it really limits what you acquire," says Bryce. He follows the one-in, one-out method of organization—for each new item he brings into the home, he lets go of something else.

As they flitted back and forth between a spacious rental house in Victoria and the compact trailer outside Joshua Tree over the next couple of years, Kelly says, "I so preferred being in the trailer, and I didn't really feel like we gave up anything, other than I couldn't have my loom there." She learned how to weave while in British Columbia and has since woven several pillows and bath towels for the RV. Kelly discovered a silver lining to this space constraint when she searched for a local art studio with a loom she could rent. She ended up finding not only a place to work but also fellow creatives to work alongside.

Since getting the trailer, the family has grown in some significant ways. A few months after finding the RV, their friends who live nearby invited them to come along as they picked out a puppy from a litter of Australian cattle dogs. Their friends didn't end up adopting one, but Kelly and Bryce couldn't resist. They brought home Sunny. Bryce expanded their full-size bed into a queen, making space for Sunny to snuggle up with them at night. They bought an unassuming house with heart-stopping views of the desert, parked the RV on the property, and lived in it as they fixed up a guest suite in the house to rent on Airbnb. Two years later, their son, Way, was born, and quite predictably changed everything.

Zipping between British Columbia and Joshua Tree wasn't as easy with a little one along for the ride, so they slowed down and moved full-time (at least for now) to the desert. They spent the temperate fall months in the trailer with both Way and Sunny—even celebrating the holidays with a creosote bush Christmas tree clipped from outside—but once the nighttime temperatures dipped below freezing, they moved into the suite in the house and have plans to start remodeling the rest of the property, with room for Kelly's loom, a home office, and space for Way to grow. The trailer isn't going anywhere. It will become a pit stop for visiting friends and family, a refuge for road-weary travelers to rest and find rejuvenation in the soul-soothing simplicity of the desert.

OPPOSITE: *On warm nights, the outdoor tub—made of local sand and a bit of concrete—is the setting for starry baths.*

cabin
crush

LEANNE FORD AND ERIK ALLEN FORD

- Laurel Canyon, Los Angeles
- 700 Square Feet
- Owned

After hiking up the forty-three steps to the front door of designer Leanne Ford's cabin, you have the nostalgic feeling that you're climbing up into a treehouse. Once inside, the home's playful energy and imaginative spirit confirms it. In between serving breakfast to Ever, the couple's now three-year-old daughter, and a visit to Buck Mason, the clothing store Leanne's husband, Erik, cofounded, the family poses atop the dining table on their deck. Ever charms the crowd by alternating between strumming on a ukulele and munching on Goldfish crackers as the camera clicks. "Welcome to our hippie commune," Leanne jokes as the family lounges on the table, dressed in shades of white and cream, a linen duvet cover standing in for a tablecloth. The vibe is laid-back but the energy, frenetic. No surprise from a couple who planned their 2017 wedding at the Bowery Hotel in just four days and had their first photo shoot for the cabin just three weeks after demo began ("We had the demo crew waiting on the driveway for when they said 'You have the keys,'" Leanne recalls).

LEFT: *"I feel like if I would have made it all perfect and easy, I would have been doing that little cabin a disservice," Leanne says. "It's been funky for one hundred years."*

OPPOSITE: *Less than 5 feet wide, this sleeping alcove is just big enough for a twin bed and a George Nelson bubble lantern suspended overhead.*

A year after relocating from LA to Pennsylvania to be near family—a move that coincided with Leanne and her brother Steve's HGTV show *Home Again with the Fords*—the couple was on the lookout for a West Coast crash pad they could flock to whenever Erik had to return to LA for work. Then, a listing for a 1924 hunting cabin in Laurel Canyon popped up on Instagram. "It was, for lack of a better word, a dump," says the designer, who was at a photo shoot in upstate New York at the time. She sent the listing to Erik, and they decided to make an offer sight unseen. "There was a full moon, so that could have been the reason—there was a full moon *and* a rainbow," she laughs. The fated property was soon theirs, and for several weeks the family lived in and worked on the rustic cabin until it looked nearly unrecognizable from the listing photos.

"The magic of paint!" Leanne says, a modest explanation for the home's radical transformation, when in reality, the magic ingredient is her inimitable sense of style and vision. Her signature look—shades of white and an abundance of texture—is in full force here. The original wall-to-wall carpeting was ripped up, exposing the worn wood floors underneath, then the entire structure was sprayed with a coat of Crisp Linen by Behr, an earthy shade of white. The masonry fireplace got a wash of watered-down alabaster grout. The entire shingled exterior and surrounding decks? More warm white paint.

"I always, always have this inner debate of 'to paint or not paint' the wood paneling—ironically, because I tell the whole world to paint it," Leanne admits. But once the paint sprayer works its wonders, she has zero regrets. "It creates new life immediately," she says, extolling the effects of white paint. "It becomes a light box . . . it makes everything more beautiful inside of it." This particular shade of white leans more traditional than modern, a fitting choice for a home with history. The biggest bonus: "It's very forgiving of design sins," she says. "Like the cabinets are old and bad; and things that we decided not to spend time and money to fix, if you paint them white, it visually goes away."

Rather than replace the wood floors, which would require more time and money and rob the cabin of some of its timeworn charm, she left the holes and scratches in place and softened the surface with white paint. "So we didn't lose anything by painting it; we just gained the lightness of it. We kept the imperfections, and because we painted everything and decorated it, the imperfections became a plus." Working with as much of the existing material as possible also lowers the environmental cost of the project, resulting in less waste and eliminating the need for new flooring.

The few elements that couldn't be painted away, like the wall that separated the former galley kitchen from the living room, were removed. In a cabin totaling only 700 square feet, the open living area still feels cozy. The central fireplace, a low-hanging linen lantern from Imprint House, layered rugs, and a pillowy sofa, designed by Leanne for Crate & Barrel and named after her daughter, all contribute to the intimacy of the space. No TV in sight, the design encourages the family to sit down, curl up, and connect.

OPPOSITE: *Panel-ready appliances fitted with painted plywood continue the rustic wood look seen throughout the cabin. The next owners can switch out the panels to match their style without having to invest in brand-new appliances. Leanne found the farmhouse table at Big Daddy's Antiques and tiled the backsplash herself using tile from Badia Design, both located in LA. When you want to design a space quickly, shopping what's in stock locally rather than waiting for shipping will speed up the project (and reduce its environmental impact).*

RIGHT: *In the primary bedroom, a pedestal table from Leanne's line at Crate & Barrel serves as a nightstand, but it could just as easily act as a side table in a living room. Versatile pieces that can fill several functions will always find a role in future homes.*

"We called it Camp California," Leanne says, recounting how they explained this home-away-from-home to Ever. "We were just on an adventure, which is what it was." Knowing that the space was temporary also granted the adults the freedom to have fun, to put practicality on the back burner. "When I'm designing for myself, I get to play," she says. One successful experiment: sponging the stone fireplace with diluted grout to veil the red tones. Leanne would periodically pause to wring out the sponge, intentionally creating drips that others might try to avoid. Shrouded in grout wash, the fireplace blends into the color palette, and because grout is easier to remove than paint, the process could potentially be reversed by the cabin's next owner.

Yet Leanne refuses to concern herself too much with her home's future lives, advising: "Don't worry about the next person; make it how you love it while you're in it, because there will be someone with a similar vision that likes what you've done to it." As someone who has always decorated her homes (including her miniscule Manhattan rental apartment straight out of college), she's a firm believer in making even a temporary home feel like you "because what happens is people think it's short-term, and then ten years later, they're still there and they haven't done anything to it."

"No matter how short-term you think it is, still create an oasis and a space that you want to spend time in and be there," she says. Take it from her—she is so good at crafting spaces everyone wants to spend time in that trudging back down the forty-three steps from the cabin out to the driveway feels like getting picked up from camp at the end of summer or being called to dinner when you're up in the treehouse. It's a little hard to leave.

ABOVE: *Hidden behind the fireplace is a semiprivate spot to check emails or read a book. For a family that's used to sprawling out in a large house, visual barriers (even if they don't provide a sound buffer) can help carve out separate spaces.*

OPPOSITE: *The handmade zellige tiles and diamond-paned window are new additions, but they both lend timeless beauty to the bathroom. Designs and materials that have been used for decades (or centuries) will never go out of style.*

Y̲ou don't have to be a minimalist to curate and declutter your home. You can have color and collections and rows of sneakers and, yes, a forest of plants—as long as they reflect your values and help you live your life as you'd like to live it. But the fact is, most of our homes contain belongings that we no longer need (and maybe never did). By letting go, we can make space for what matters most to us, we can find time we didn't know we had, and we can love where we are a little more fully.

A good portion of the clutter we hold on to are items that don't serve our lives at the present moment. There are old cell phones we haven't donated and clothes that haven't fit in years. It's hard to let go of the past. And then there's the skateboard we wanted to learn how to ride but never did, and the gown we planned to wear to some elegant event we're still waiting to be invited to. It's hard to let go of potential futures. Parting with these items can feel a little bit like grieving—for past selves, for life changes. But in the end, editing what we own can help us gain far more than we lose, whether that's physical space to hang out, exercise, or dance, or mental space for more calm, clarity, or productivity. Not to mention the time we'll reclaim when we have fewer belongings to maintain and organize. Paring back can actually make our lives feel more abundant.

Refocus on Your Priorities

Write out a list of the items or activities you want to prioritize in your home (then have your partner, kids, or roommates do the same). You can list physical belongings, like your surfboard, or concepts, like "room for creative expression." Then, like any good work of art, leave some negative space. You can't cook without clear counters, and it's difficult to practice yoga without room to roll out a mat. So how do you make space for what matters most? Pay attention to what's missing from your list or falls down near the bottom. Make sure these low-priority items aren't demanding too much real estate. If you don't care much about clothing, you probably don't need a closet overflowing with options. If you rarely cook, reconsider all those appliances cluttering your kitchen cabinets. There's a reason some space-strapped New Yorkers store sweaters in the oven and jeans in the freezer—it's all about making space for whatever feeds your soul. Keep in mind that some items take up more space in our lives than just their physical forms. For example, Leanne has left a television out of her living room (page 28), but the shelves are stocked with books, records, paintbrushes, and a Polaroid camera, suggesting some alternative uses for the time and attention one might otherwise devote to a TV. "I really wanted this to feel like a creatively inspiring cabin," she explains. "A blank slate . . . a beautiful light box with good music playing that is going to inspire you to think creatively and do some art, do some music, and play." How we choose to fill our homes will determine how we live in them.

OPPOSITE: *By squeezing a massive dining table into the small cabin, Leanne prioritizes communal gathering space.*

Sort Memories

Whenever decluttering is discussed, you'll likely hear the refrain, "It's just stuff." But for many of us, the objects in our lives hold meaning beyond their utilitarian value—if they didn't, they would be infinitely easier to part with. There's a reason boxing up all possessions that remind someone of their ex is an enduring trope whenever a couple breaks up in a movie or TV show; our belongings are keepers of memories. They help tell our stories. Depending upon what you're organizing, decluttering can be an emotional process, so grant yourself the space for that. There may be many things you simply can't part with for sentimental reasons—that's to be expected—but here are some strategies for preserving the memories without holding on to the objects themselves:

1. Take a photo of the item (and even print it out).
2. Clip just a portion of an old favorite garment, like the lace hem of a dress.
3. Write out a memory associated with the object in vivid detail.
4. Store these written memories and photographs in a file (physical, digital, or both) so you can revisit them whenever you like. This will also help anyone else who discovers these files in the future understand their significance.

Embrace Change

Between the clothes that no longer fit (either our bodies or our sense of style), the hobbies we've outgrown, and the kitchen appliances we never use, a lot of clutter accumulates because it's difficult for us to adapt to change. It can be hard to admit that you haven't knit in a decade, even when you used to love it, or that the juicer you bought during a health kick hasn't seen a carrot in years. Change is tough, but by letting go of these items, you can make space for your life as you live it right now—and the clothes, hobbies, and kitchen appliances that make you happy.

Cut the Aspirational Clutter

While some clutter is stalled on past versions of ourselves, other clutter stands for imagined future selves that we struggle to let go of. This is my Achilles' heel of organization. There's the DIY espadrilles kit that I held on to for five years, and the pottery wheel I used twice, and that copy of *War and Peace* I got when I was twelve and still haven't finished. It took me years to accept that I may never become the type of person who crochets their own sandals, but I felt lighter the second I gave the kit away to someone else who will actually use it. What future selves are you holding on to? The one who snowboards or paints? Ask yourself: (1) Will you realistically use those items in the future?; (2) Do they still reflect your goals?; and (3) Do they make you feel inspired or guilty? Depending upon your answers, letting go can free up valuable space for other belongings, pursuits, and interests that *will* enrich your life.

Start with the Easy Stuff

Just deciding to declutter is oftentimes the hardest step. To gain momentum, set a timer for ten minutes and begin with some obvious items, ones without any emotional attachment. Toss out or recycle these belongings without a second thought:

- Chipped dishware and mugs
- Expired toiletries, makeup, and food
- Junk mail and catalogs
- Old plastic food containers without lids
- Socks with holes

OPPOSITE: *Collected trinkets, Polaroid pictures, and antique busts form a layered history on Leanne's shelves—proof that even minimalist homes should leave space for treasured objects. The mushroom side table was hand-carved by Beck and Cap.*

Pretend You're Moving

There are a lot of different decluttering strategies that can work; the key is identifying the one that works for you. For example, Bryce follows the one-in, one-out rule to maintain equilibrium—for each new item he brings in, he gets rid of a similar item. When you haven't wrangled the chaos in a while and feel that your home is in need of a complete overhaul, try this trick: Pretend you're moving. If you're in a rental or space that you don't plan to live in forever, this shouldn't be too difficult to imagine. Plus, you'll feel more prepared when you eventually do move out. Ask yourself: "Would I take this with me if I was moving?" If you would go through the effort to pack the item, lug it to your new home, and unpack it, then it's worth its weight. The effort that goes into moving makes us more ruthless declutterers, helping us get down to brass tacks and keep only what matters most.

Avoid the Landfill

Only a very small amount of clutter should be destined for the trash can or recycling bin—like the piles of mail that can be shredded and recycled. (Then switch to online billing and cancel unnecessary catalogs.) Clothes, home decor, and electronics in good condition can be donated. Just check with the organization first to see which items they accept, so you can avoid making your clutter someone else's burden. List items for sale (or free) on online platforms, such as Facebook Marketplace and Craigslist. If you live in a city, let your neighbors help. Living on a street that gets a fair bit of foot traffic, I regularly leave out a bin of items marked "Free" on the sidewalk—everything is typically gone in under an hour. Take clothing and textiles that are in bad condition to a fabric recycling center, then bring broken or unusable electronics to your local drop-off site (find one at Earth911.com).

Invest in Better

To stop the cycle of clutter, rethink what you bring into your home. Choosing durable furniture, decor, and clothes that you love will save cheap, low-quality pieces from the landfill. This may require an initial investment in money or time. Well-made furniture will cost more but last longer, and you can likely find a deal on a resale platform or at an antique store, even if it takes some patience to find the right piece. Skip any furniture that's too trendy or that you suspect won't fit your style long-term (leave trends for smaller details, like throw pillow covers).

OPPOSITE: *Kelly found the water dispenser at a local thrift store for $15.*

Chapter 2
TIDY

serenity
in the
city

FIONA BYRNE

- Lower East Side, Manhattan
- 400 Square Feet
- Rented

W hen most people move out of their home of sixteen years, there are towering stacks of papers to sift through, neglected pasta machines and panini presses to donate, and a sizable mountain of ill-fitting, out-of-date clothing to contend with. But Fiona Byrne is not most people. "When I moved out of that apartment, I didn't have any organizing to do," says the designer and writer about her former Lower East Side apartment. "I went through the whole apartment knowing I was going to move, being like, 'Well, what can I get together to put in boxes?' And everything was already together. It took me no time."

This method is particularly convenient when it comes to clothing, because the very act of getting dressed each day is a process of curation. Fiona had a navy sailor-style top she at first adored, but as her tastes evolved and her personal palette solidified to just black, white, and red, she suddenly couldn't stomach navy. Whenever she tried on the top, her immediate reaction—"I don't feel like myself"—served as a gut check. Without hesitation, she parted with the top, along with any other piece of clothing that didn't pass the test—no need to wait for a big move. When life is short and space is limited, we only have time for clothing that fits and feels like us.

One happy result of this continual editing process was that Fiona's small step-in closet contained her clothing for all seasons. Off-season items stored near the ceiling were switched out as needed. Come springtime, a clear hatbox full of bikinis replaced the hatbox full of gloves. Pull-out shoe racks from the Container Store spanned from floor to ceiling, maximizing every inch of vertical space and preventing shoes from littering the floor. On the opposite wall, a set of wall-mounted wire baskets meant to hold spices and condiments in the kitchen was repurposed as a catchall for clutches and purses. By adhering to a strict color palette, both in her wardrobe and in her decor, Fiona owns fewer, higher-quality pieces, knowing that every single item will mix and match well together.

OPPOSITE: *A modular system of organizers lets Fiona tailor her storage to her wardrobe. She calculated exactly how many pull-out shelves she needed for her shoes and how many drawers for socks and accessories. Since the entire system is easily unscrewed from the wall, Fiona took it with her to her next apartment.*

"I like nice things, I just don't like a lot of things," explains Fiona, who applies this ethos to her home decor as well. An Irish expat who moved to New York City in the early aughts to pursue a career in journalism, Fiona was thrilled to have an apartment that looked like the ones on TV, complete with wood floors (carpets were on-trend in Ireland at the time) and an American-style peephole à la *Friends*. For the first several years, she shared the apartment with a roommate and outfitted her bedroom (which later became the living room) with Ikea pieces, many of which she slowly upgraded over the years. While some renters hesitate to splurge on furniture, Fiona has recently adopted a different approach. "I want to have pieces that are valuable and that I can resell if I move or if I want to change for something else, so I'm not trying to sell a sofa that nobody wants. At a certain point, you have to buy investment pieces," she says.

ABOVE: *To channel hotel vibes, Fiona wrapped her bed in white sateen sheets. White bedding and bath towels are counterintuitively easy to keep clean—they can be washed together without fear of dyes running and bleached to remove stains and prevent dinginess. Injections of color come in the form of artwork by Cacho Falcon and a sculptural Modeline of California lamp that Fiona spray-painted out on her fire escape.*

OPPOSITE: *To introduce some architectural interest, Fiona hired a contractor to affix picture frame molding to the white walls. In her new apartment, she faced her fear of the compound miter saw (which she snagged online for $76) and tackled the job herself, securing molding onto the walls of her bedroom using heavy-duty adhesive, then caulking around the edges and painting the entire wall and molding. "It looks so amazing," she says. "I probably would have done a more elaborate molding in the old place if I knew it was that easy."*

In her home office, a snug alcove off the entryway, one iconic Ikea piece continued to make the cut: a Kallax shelving unit. To outfit the grid of shelves, Fiona painted sixteen wooden boxes white, only to discover that the round handle cutouts bothered her. Turning her pet peeve into a full-blown design statement, she ordered circular decals off Etsy to stick everywhere—on the walls, bins, books. The room resembled a Yayoi Kusama art installation, yet on moving day, removal was as easy as peeling off a sticker. The main storage hub in her home, these bins hid it all: hardware, documents, toiletries. The entire wall was secretly a hive of household storage, yet the camouflaged boxes maintained the appearance of a calm, uncluttered home office.

Borrowing some storage space from the office allowed Fiona to open up her kitchen. After getting the property owner's go-ahead, she removed the upper cabinets, transferring the hardware previously stashed above the fridge to a polka-dot bin and relocating her dishware to the new floating shelves. The lower cabinets provided just enough space to hide the pots, pans, and blender of a not-so-avid cook, while the shelving above offered valuable display space for a voracious art collector's finds. A trio of Warhol-inspired soup canisters sat on one shelf, while a taxidermy puffin collected during a trip to the Reykjavík Fashion Festival roosted on another.

OPPOSITE: *The wallpaper mural, a splashy pattern in primary colors by Drop It Modern, disrupts the monochromatic kitchen.*

RIGHT: *Polka dots help the storage unit blend into the background, while the desk (an acrylic console from CB2) disappears completely.*

Determining the right shades required careful consideration. "I suppose it must have something to do with the chaos and the filth outside that I just wanted to make the most serene place," Fiona reflects.

To brighten up the warren of tiny rooms, Fiona painted every surface in shades of white—Decorator's White by Benjamin Moore for the walls and ceiling, Extra White by Sherwin-Williams for the floor. Determining the right shades required careful consideration. The south-facing apartment receives warm light, so a cool shade with a drop of gray undertone read as a crisp, pure white. All the temperature-taking was worth it—the effect was a clean slate, punctuated by pieces with personality. "I suppose it must have something to do with the chaos and the filth outside that I just wanted the most serene place," Fiona reflects. Over time, the spirited neighborhood would crescendo to a fever pitch, precipitating the designer's move to a quiet enclave of Brooklyn. But for as long as she could, she carved out her own tranquil slice of the city.

OPPOSITE: *The Chasing Paper wallpaper, featuring illustrations by Carolyn Suzuki, comes in peel-and-stick and traditional styles, so both renters and homeowners can dress up their walls. To freshen up the formerly white grout, Fiona used four dark gray grout pens to color within the lines. If you're saving up for a bathroom remodel, grout pens can change the color of the grout and help seal it until you're ready to retile. The clear shower curtain makes the tiny bathroom feel as spacious as possible.*

a room
of
her own

KATE HAMILTON GRAY

- Carroll Gardens, Brooklyn
- 500 Square Feet
- Rented

"If you ask my mom, she would say that I'm not an organized person," interior designer Kate Hamilton Gray says with a laugh, "but I really do keep this place organized," she insists. Her mother's intrinsic tidiness may have (arguably) skipped a generation, but Kate inherited her father's more studied dedication to the cause. "My dad is a ship captain, so order and the sort of discipline that goes with being on boats is something that is ingrained in me a little bit." The same lessons apply to living in a small apartment, she explains: "You have to put everything back in its place; it keeps you honest." Otherwise, the chaos unfolds quickly.

The key to staying organized when it doesn't come effortlessly? Implementing systems she can actually stick to. Shaker peg rails line the walls of her bedroom, holding her bathrobe, whatever pieces of clothing are in heavy rotation at the moment, a framed photograph, a wicker basket full of hair ties, a circular mirror on a delicate chain. She'll rest a watercolor across the top of two wooden pegs, or she'll clear everything off and hang her laundry to dry. Outside her apartment, more peg rails line the walls of the stair landing, which Kate has to herself because she lives on the upper floor of a two-story row house. Standing in for a coat closet, the peg rails stash jackets and scarves that Kate can quickly grab on her way to client meetings or site visits. With no clothes hangers to contend with, no folding or sorting necessary, it's a system that's easy to maintain.

ABOVE: *Kate studied furniture design at the Rhode Island School of Design; she carved the wooden stump side table for a class. The sofa was reupholstered in a Rebecca Atwood fabric; the small-scale pattern adds subtle texture to the room. Renters, take note: To avoid hardwiring (and hiring an electrician),* *Kate chose a plug-in sconce. Instead of framing the charcoal landscape sketch and drilling a hole in the wall to attach it, pushpins leave discreet marks that won't need to be repaired before she moves out. And rather than put up shelving, a wooden ladder leaning against the wall holds bags and blankets.*

When asked whether she's an intuitively tidy person, the designer shakes her head emphatically. "No, I have a lot of baskets." In the living room, a woven basket stows skeins of yarn for knitting; in the kitchen, another stores colorful cloth napkins; in the bedroom, a laundry basket hides bulky sweaters Kate wears regularly. "It's good to have places where you can tidy up—even if it's temporary tidying—and then on the weekends, you really get into it," she says. On hectic weekdays, she'll toss knitting projects and sweaters into the assorted baskets to sort on weekends when life slows down. Rather than overcommit to an ambitious organization system she'll abandon within a week, baskets and peg rails help even those who aren't naturally neat live the organized life. The minimal effort pays dividends. "When things are clean and tidy in here, it's just blissful. I feel really calm and peaceful."

While working on the apartment, she balanced a space that matches her style with one that satisfies her storage needs. The property owner, who is also Kate's friend, agreed to invest in a kitchen remodel if Kate would design and oversee the project. To save money, she preserved the kitchen's original layout, keeping the stove and sink in the same locations, but she removed all the old cabinets, which were so caked with layers of paint that the doors would stick and the drawers would clank. She swapped out the lower cabinets with prefabricated ones from a local vendor that actually cost less than Ikea options.

A long open shelf replaced the upper cabinets, leaving a blank wall to showcase a subdued, leaf-scattered wallpaper by Rebecca Atwood, a designer and Kate's friend, who used to live in the garden apartment downstairs. Unlike closed cabinets, which quickly devolve into a tower of take-out containers and souvenir mugs, the open shelving prompts Kate to declutter unrelentingly. She has whittled down her dishware to a capsule collection of glasses and ceramics that she eats and drinks from daily. "I love the little tin ceiling in the space, and I thought it was nice to keep things open. But in the spirit of storage, I think it was being a little bit optimistic," Kate admits. After living with the setup for a while, she

ABOVE: *To keep the counter organized, an enamel tray corrals the essentials: salt, pepper, and olive oil.*

embrace your space

introduced a glass-front Ikea cabinet on the other side of the kitchen, which serves as an improvised pantry.

When selecting furniture and decor, Kate avoided buying anything that was too specific to the space, opting instead for versatile pieces that could work in future homes as well. For custom pieces, such as the bench that runs along the back wall of the apartment, she sourced inexpensive supplies. Kate bought plywood and two-by-fours at Home Depot, and the builder who worked on the kitchen constructed the bench for her. The small investment has paid off, both in terms of storage and enjoyment. Underneath the bench, striped curtains hide a toolbox, a bin of carpet samples, and the internet modem. At golden hour when light flows in through the back windows, the bench seat, topped with a soft sheepskin, is Kate's favorite spot to sit and work at her laptop or sketch out designs in a notebook.

ABOVE: *A Windsor chair hugs close to a pedestal table, forming a compact dining area outside the kitchen. Vibrant artwork by Charlotte Hallberg energizes the otherwise neutral space.*

Kate also put her personal touch on the bathroom by hand-painting a star pattern on the wall. Inspired by the whimsical bathrooms embellished by artist Saul Steinberg–featuring nudes painted on the sides of clawfoot tubs and tree branches brushed on shower tiles–Kate wanted a space that didn't take itself too seriously. The cherry on top: It's easy to switch up whenever she's ready for a change, and it can be painted over when it's time to move out. "For me, it's worth it to spend a little money, and if you have to repaint your bathroom before you leave, big deal," she shrugs. Living on her own for the first time, Kate had complete freedom to add these playful details. "I think it's the first place that's an expression of my own personality and is a space that feels like it is mine."

A few months ago, when her friend moved out downstairs, Kate had the opportunity to claim the garden apartment in the building, which boasts more space and private access to the backyard but doesn't get as much sunlight. Kate couldn't wrap her head around leaving the bright and happy home she's created for herself. "I just love my little space up here. I'm all tucked in, and it's cozy." She decided to stay. For now, she's found her spot in the sun.

OPPOSITE: *Kate painted the stars using an $8 sample pot of Lulworth Blue by Farrow & Ball.*

RIGHT: *"I look for these heart rocks whenever I'm by the ocean," Kate says. Her collection contains specimens from travels abroad, as well as visits to family in Rhode Island and Maine. "I spend a lot of time in Rhode Island, and the ocean and nature are really important to me," she says, "so having a space in the city that is affordable allows me the flexibility to spend time elsewhere." Living in a small space expands, rather than limits, her world.*

There is no one-size-fits-all answer to home organization. The best storage checks at least three boxes: It fits your stuff, it fits your space, and it fits your style. Once you've decluttered what you don't need, take stock of what you own. Your belongings and daily routine should guide the storage you select. Versatile organizers that can adapt to evolving needs—think adjustable drawer dividers or an expandable accordion-style coatrack—will work in your current home and the next one.

Give Everything a Home

When you move into a new place, there are some questions to answer: Where do the mugs belong? And the scissors? How about camping gear? If you skip those decisions—or if everyone in your household hasn't agreed to them—it will always be a struggle to find what you're looking for. It's not too late! Reevaluate the items you frequently spend time searching for. Step one: Decide on a spot for each of those belongings (and make sure your partner, roommates, or kids know, too). Step two: Store the item so it's easy to reach when you need it. The right organizers can help with that.

Double the Storage You Do Have

Before you buy new bins, baskets, and bookcases, optimize the storage already built into your home.

Closets: It's time to fake a custom closet. First, evaluate what you own. Exactly how many shirts and jeans do you typically fold? How many dresses, blouses, and jackets do you hang up? Taking an actual count of your clothing—not just a guess—will indicate precisely how much room you should devote to shelves versus closet rods. To instantly double your closet space, mount two closet rods, one above the other (as Fiona did in her closet, page 36). Measure your clothing to determine the vertical spacing between the two rods, leaving at least 3 feet of hanging space between them. Swapping out bulky clothes hangers for a matching set of slim, nonslip ones will dramatically increase the amount of clothing your closet can hold.

Clip on an over-the-door organizer to sort small accessories, such as gloves, hats, belts, and scarves. One with clear pockets lets you find your sunglasses or slippers at a glance. Invest in organizers, shoe racks, and hangers that not only fit your current closet but also match your style—you'll want to take them with you when you move.

Drawers: Without dividers, every drawer risks becoming a junk drawer. Measure your kitchen drawers carefully, then order a cutlery tray. A set of adjustable drawer dividers can sort cloth napkins and cooking tools in one drawer, and separate scissors, tape, and paper clips in another. These adaptable dividers can come along with you wherever you go.

Kitchen cabinets: Most cabinets contain some underutilized vertical space. Introducing a shelf riser can help. Stash mugs or small bowls below, glasses or dessert plates up top. An expandable tiered spice rack saves space while the stadium seating design helps you find the paprika without lifting up each bottle to read the label.

Shelves: To max out shelf space in a closet, install shelves all the way from floor to ceiling. Stash off-season clothing near the top—just switch out the shorts and T-shirts for sweaters and scarves as the seasons change—and let the lower shelves prevent the predictable shoe pile on the closet floor. Use shelf dividers to sort stacks of folded jeans and sweaters and keep them from toppling over. If you have open space below a shelf, slide on an undershelf basket that can hold a few more folded shirts or jeans.

Go High and Low

Unused space is most often found high up near the ceiling and down low, hidden under furniture. To maximize vertical space:

> Add higher shelves in your closet for luggage or off-season clothing.
> Secure a shelf above the bathroom door or toilet to hold towels or toilet paper.
> Suspend a tiered hanging fruit basket from your kitchen ceiling.
> Attach a caddy to the showerhead to keep soap and shampoo within reach.
> Store serveware and infrequently used small appliances in bins above your kitchen cabinets.

If your bed frame or sofa is elevated off the floor, slide some low-profile organizers underneath. Measure the clearance carefully (taking any rugs into consideration) before you shop for storage. Let breathable underbed bins stash off-season clothing or spare bedding. Remember: Lidded bins keep everything dust-free.

BELOW: *In Kate's kitchen, closed cabinets conceal cooking supplies and open shelving shows off ceramics.*

Work with Your Routine

When integrating storage into your home, consider first how you live in the space. If clothing piles up on a chair in your bedroom or mail collects on the kitchen counter, let these habits guide your storage choices—attach wall hooks above the bedroom chair and set a paper sorter on the counter. With storage coordinated to your routine, you won't have to go out of your way to stay organized.

Mix Open and Closed Storage

Not everything we own is worthy of display. Open shelves are great for showing off your favorite belongings—whether that means ceramics in the kitchen or books in the living room—but closed cabinets, drawers, dressers, woven bins, and baskets can help hide the rest. Cabinets with frosted or reeded glass fronts lend a feeling of openness, while concealing any clutter that lies behind. For those who love the look of open storage in a kitchen, keep an eye out for cooking tools, dishware, and pots and pans that deliver both form and function. A vintage bottle opener doubles as art on a pegboard while handmade plates deserve to be admired in glass-front cabinets. Plus, you'll want to keep these special pieces for years to come.

Fill in the Gaps

If you're renting or saving up for a remodel, there may be gaps between appliances and cabinets in your kitchen. To squeeze in a little more storage, measure the opening, then search for a rolling storage cart that matches the dimensions. A marble cart with open shelving is a pretty display for copper pots or ceramic serving bowls, while a cart with a butcher block top adds a small but much-appreciated work surface to the room.

Maximize Wall Space

Call it the law of home design gravity, but furniture, lamps, and baskets tend to clutter the floor while empty walls float above. To introduce storage you won't trip over, work the walls. Consider mounting a shelving unit on a living room wall for books, vases, and your record player. In the kitchen, a metal rail and a set of S-hooks can store cooking tools, trivets, and dish towels. A wall-mounted desk with a folding laptop ledge presents a space-saving solution for those who work from home. The design encourages you to keep your work surface clear, and closing it up at the end of each day will help you disconnect from work. When attaching any storage designed to hold heavy items, be sure to screw directly into the wall studs (a store-bought stud finder can help).

Choose Furniture with Built-In Storage

Let a vintage storage chest serve as your coffee table; line a breakfast nook with bench seating equipped with cubbies; select a sofa whose cushions lift up, revealing compartments for spare blankets. Furniture that doubles as storage reduces the number of pieces you need in a room, preventing it from feeling cluttered. But because these pieces tend to be bulky, counterbalance them with delicate furniture that adds lightness to the space, such as a narrow console table or a coffee table with hairpin legs.

OPPOSITE: *A worn vintage cabinet provides patina and a spot to stow odds and ends in roommates Julia, Paris, and Tori's home.*

Make It Match Your Style

Especially in a small space, you'll need to weave storage into your design plan. One method: Source budget-friendly pieces from big-box stores, then add your own DIY spin. In Kate's apartment, she spruced up a basic pine dresser from Ikea with a coat of green-gray paint and new knobs. You can also personalize the storage you already own. Line a drawer with colorful contact paper or decorate a closet with removable wallpaper. These spaces may be functional first, but there's no reason why they shouldn't coordinate with your decor. If you choose to splurge on storage, consider pieces that you're likely to take with you from place to place and that will fit your aesthetic long-term, such as a freestanding vintage armoire for the traditionalist or a Vitsoe shelving unit for the midcentury-modern lover. Even if they don't end up working in your next home, these timeless pieces will be easy to resell.

Construct Faux Built-Ins

If you have any alcoves in your home (which urban apartments with awkward layouts often do), convert them into storage space. Install shelves that span the width of the nook, like Julia, Tori, and Paris did in their kitchen (pictured opposite.) For a faux built-in look, hang up floating shelves, then paint the shelves and the walls of the alcove the same color. An entire wall of cabinets can blend seamlessly into the space, while providing ample storage. If you're not about to splurge on custom cabinets, consider a row of Pax wardrobes from Ikea—when embellished with molding, painted to match, and adorned with hardware, they'll look like they've always been there. Attach crown molding and brush on some paint, and a series of Billy bookcases can produce the same effect.

OPPOSITE: *Roommates Julia, Paris, and Tori fashioned a collective closet out of $150 worth of plywood, brackets, and clothing rods.*

Chapter 3
TINY

studio of
splendors

NATASHA NYANIN

- Upper West Side, Manhattan
- 350 Square Feet
- Rented

For the first year and a half that Natasha Nyanin lived in her studio apartment, the only sliver of counter space was a 20 x 25-inch slab tucked between the sink and the stove. "I had a glazed goose Christmas Eve dinner during that period," she says, as if still in disbelief. To make up for her tiny "New York-size" oven, she got creative and snuck into one of the unoccupied units in her building to use the kitchen. "I think I'm the reason they now always lock the doors of the empty units," she confesses with a laugh. Possessing a natural gift for both cooking and hosting, Natasha refuses to let limited square footage stop her from entertaining. In fact, when collaborating with interior designer Nina Blair on the look of her home, Natasha insisted on a rectangular dining table that could seat up to six because she prioritized a proper setting for dinner parties.

"The next time I hosted Christmas Eve dinner, the kitchen was done, so it was a different experience, having more space," she says. The formerly empty wall on the right-hand side of the kitchen was outfitted with maple shelves from Semihandmade, a worthy perch to display Natasha's extensive assortment of cookware collected from around the world. Shigaraki ware teacups from Tokyo mingle with copper tagines from Fès. Below, cabinets were modified to fit the narrow galley kitchen (the standard 24-inch depth was truncated to just 18 inches) and a faux marble counter by Stone Coat Countertops—the result of pouring epoxy over MDF and blending in ribbons of contrasting color to imitate natural veining—spans the length of the room. Invaluable as it is for meal prep, the extra counter space didn't magically prevent all future holiday mishaps. "This year, my croquembouche tower collapsed because the caramel wouldn't set," she laments. Did that stop her friends from devouring every last bite of deconstructed pastry puff? Take one guess.

LEFT: *Some surprisingly low-cost DIY projects lend the galley kitchen its high-end look. Inspired by designer Brady Tolbert's former LA rental, Natasha covered the floor with vinyl peel-and-stick tiles following a checkerboard pattern. The grand total: just $40. The imitation marble counters were crafted by pouring and drizzling epoxy over MDF; each kit from Stone Coat Countertops costs about $125 and covers 20 square feet. Renters, pour it over plywood cut to fit snugly over the existing counter; homeowners, apply it directly onto old laminate counters to get the faux marble effect.*

embrace your space

A visit to Natasha's apartment is also a feast for the eyes. Stepping inside the studio feels like peeking inside a jewel box, each item a gem to discover. Nestled between two upholstered slipper chairs, a slender table sculpted from brass and rose-toned marble rests after a long journey. Having admired a similar table at jeweler Bia Daidone's studio in São Paulo a few years ago, Natasha commissioned her to make a replica. The delicate piece was hand-delivered, first hopping a flight from Brazil to Miami with the jewelry designer, then transferred to a friend of Natasha's for transport to Manhattan, and ultimately landing in its current home on the Upper West Side. Now, the side table not only is a beautiful object to behold but also tells a story.

ABOVE: *The art over the sofa was bought in Accra, Ghana, for $40; the agate chess set was found at a souk in Marrakech and hauled home in Natasha's carry-on bag.*

This was part of Natasha's plan for her place. "I wanted to fill it with little things that were interesting and that told stories and reminded me of people, reminded me of places and things, or feelings or poems or emotions. It probably doesn't help that I'm a person who has a great many different interests, so there's a lot that I try to capture at once." Brimming with storied possessions, such as an antique Ashanti stool and an English brass inkwell from the late 1800s, the small apartment holds a rich history.

The child of diplomats—born in London, raised in Ghana—Natasha is a creative consultant and writer who frequently covers travel, a career that helps inform (and provides fodder for) her global approach to home decorating. "I wanted to look around and be in love with my surroundings, and I wanted to be able to travel through my surroundings," she says. Some of the pieces are souvenirs acquired on trips and carried home, others were sourced online from vendors around the world. Several of her well-traveled belongings show the marks of a lengthy voyage. When she ordered a trio of alabaster vases, which she first spotted at a hotel in Morocco, one vessel arrived broken. The company offered to replace it, but instead, Natasha salvaged it with kintsugi, an ancient method of repairing broken pottery with powdered gold blended into lacquer, a technique that she describes as "emblematic of my life philosophy." A believer in wabi-sabi, a Japanese aesthetic and worldview focused on the acceptance of imperfection and impermanence, Natasha has curated a trove of treasures that are meant to be lived with rather than admired from afar. In her world, there's no use crying over a chipped vase or a collapsed croquembouche—these imperfections only add to their beauty.

OPPOSITE: *Sumptuous materials—a blush velvet sofa, a Milo Baughman brass bar cart, and a ribbed glass decanter—elevate everyday acts, such as watching TV and mixing a drink, to an art form. In fact, even Natasha's TV is art: The Samsung Frame displays a favorite painting whenever she isn't shouting at a tennis match or screening a movie with her film club. Natasha has a knack for aggrandizing the ordinary. In a world of texting, she still keeps handwritten correspondence, putting calligraphy pen to paper and securing each envelope with a burgundy wax seal.*

"This is where I live now and I want to enjoy my life now, even if I am hoping for more in the future," Natasha says.

A wabi-sabi-inspired appreciation for impermanence also plays into Natasha's decision to invest in her rental space. After referencing Amy Sedaris's home tour with *The Cut*, in which the comedian recommends thinking of your security deposit as a "personality fee," Natasha reveals she has crunched the numbers on her personality: "I worked it out; if I live here for five years, it's an extra $30 per month of rent." It's a fee that, to her, feels well worth it. "We tend to be so future focused, like 'When I have my own house' or 'When I have my big space,' or whatever it is, but life is fleeting and you don't know what's going to happen, so I try to really practice that presence whatever the situation may be," she explains. "This is where I live now and I want to enjoy my life now, even if I am hoping for more in the future."

OPPOSITE: *Natasha embraced the lack of natural light in her bathroom, painting the walls Blackest by Clare and regrouting the subway tiles below deep charcoal—a forgiving design choice that allows her to scrub grout lines less often. Luxe little details, such as the brass and porcelain faucet handles, glimmer against the dramatic backdrop. Not about to splurge on a brand-new sink, shower, or toilet? Replacing the faucet, handles, and showerhead will make it look like you did.*

a *stylish* sanctuary

LISA LU

- Chelsea, Manhattan
- 350 Square Feet
- Rented

"It's actually one of those New York urban legends," Lisa Lu says, recounting the serendipitous circumstances that led her to a highly coveted rent-stabilized apartment in Chelsea. Ten years ago, she was newly single with a budding career in fashion PR and an unhappy roommate situation. Then, Lisa's friend had an appointment with her hair stylist, who mentioned he was looking for someone to take over the lease on his apartment. "I went to see it and agreed to move in the same day. You always hear these stories about apartments getting passed down in New York, and you never think it's going to happen."

Eight years later, the cozy studio was still "perfectly nice," yet Lisa couldn't shake the feeling that something was missing. Then the COVID-19 pandemic struck, and she suddenly found herself home 24/7. She knew it was time to infuse more of her style into the space. "I guess there's something to be said about captivity breeding creativity," she laughs.

Prior to what would become a whirlwind month-long makeover, Lisa had never used a

drill before, and she would hire a pro for any task that required putting holes in the wall. "It just feels so permanent," she explains. After weeks of tripping over the bar shelving unit that sat on her living room floor—a project put on pause because no one could come install it in the midst of lockdown—Lisa decided to take matters (and power tools) into her own hands. Hanging the bar above her dining table instilled in her the confidence to tackle other project ideas that had been percolating in her head for years.

"When I started, everything in the kitchen was this sad-looking custard color, from the tiles to the walls to the cabinets. It was super depressing," she says. She cheered up the walls with a coat of white paint, applied stick-on subway tiles directly on top of the dingy backsplash, wrapped the counter with marble contact paper, and painted the cabinet fronts a deep blue green. For this renter, reversibility was key. She decided to paint just the cabinet fronts (which were previously painted white) and left the wooden bases as is. For several days, the cabinet doors rested on painter's pyramids, hovering inches above the floor and forming a precarious maze Lisa had to tiptoe around each time she trekked to the bathroom.

RIGHT: *A counter-height table serves as a desk by day, extra dinner prep space by night. When it's not working a double shift, the nook feels like a vacation, with its well-stocked West Elm bar and a transportive print by Ted Gushue.*

OPPOSITE: *Perhaps the most impressive aspect of Lisa's rental kitchen makeover—besides the fact that it took her less than two weeks and cost less than $350—is that every detail can be reset to its original state when she moves out. The adhesive subway tile and the marble contact paper on the counter will peel away. The cabinet fronts brushed with blue-green paint (Backdrop's Saturday on Sunday) will be reversed with a coat of white paint. The brass hardware will be unscrewed and maybe even packed up for Lisa's next place.*

Come move-out day, she may have to repaint the cabinets and peel off the stick-on subway tile, but for now, she's savoring how much better meals taste when cooked in a well-designed kitchen. "One of my proudest accomplishments is I made Jonathan Waxman's roast chicken and crisp baked potatoes from Barbuto, one of my favorite restaurants," which satisfied a craving while the restaurant was temporarily closed. "And I'm always asking my mom how to make Vietnamese dishes when I miss her cooking." An exclusive invite to dinner at Lisa's place is one of the hottest tickets in town—for those willing to brave the sixth-floor walk-up. "It's not really a party pad for me," she says. "There is something about it that's very personal, so I'll share it with a select few people."

Paint plays a big role throughout the apartment, both to set the tone and to visually separate the studio. In her job in fashion PR, Lisa relies on clothing in neutral colors and simple shapes to help her keep a low profile at shows and events, so home decorating offers a chance to let loose. "When it comes to my apartment and interior design, that's a place where I can express myself and play with colors that I love seeing on the runway that I would never really wear myself."

OPPOSITE: *The bathroom glows as sunlight reflects off the warm, luminous pink paint. The earthy hue is broken up by a watery art print by Angela Mckay. Lisa ordered the decorative molding that adorns the door off Etsy, and each adhesive-backed piece arrived cut to size and ready to stick on—no saw or nails necessary. Once cloaked in paint, this architectural detail appears to have always been there. After discovering that the light fixture above the medicine cabinet was permanently bonded to the wall, Lisa gave it the Midas touch*

with antique gold Rub 'n Buff, a metallic wax with the power to recast nickel as brass.

ABOVE: *Throughout the studio, storage hides in plain sight. The vintage trunk, repurposed as a coffee table, acts as the "junk drawer" for the apartment, concealing a jumble of tools, crafting supplies, and wrapping paper. A row of white Bestå cabinets hovers near the ceiling, stashing off-season clothing so Lisa can forgo a storage unit.*

Color blocking also serves a practical purpose: It compartmentalizes the studio without the need for walls or dividers, which would only make the 350 square feet feel smaller. "The best thing you can do is embrace that it's one space," Lisa recommends to anyone struggling with the layout of a studio. "It's all about creating different zones within that space that function for the way that you live, and you can totally do that without walls by using rugs and paint and art." The dining area feels distinct from the adjoining bedroom, thanks to a coat of Tanlines by Backdrop. The bathroom transports you far away from Manhattan with its rich coral walls (36 Hours in Marrakesh by Backdrop) and star-patterned stick-on floor decals covering the drab tiles below.

The various colors help delineate zones, but they also complement one another. "When your apartment is one room and you can see everything at any given time, it's especially important for the palette to be cohesive. I think taking a piece of art or some other object as a focus that you can pull colors from is one way for everything to tie all together," Lisa says. For her, the skateboard decks above her bed are the point from which the design scheme flows—every color in the apartment stems from those decks.

In total, the studio makeover tallied under $2,000. It's a sum Lisa won't get back when she moves out, but in terms of happiness, she assures us the ROI is through the roof. "For me, it's made such an incredible difference in my state of mind whenever I'm at home," she says. "I'm so happy to be in that space. It's like night and day from before."

RIGHT: *An illustration of rapper Cam'Ron by Yung Lenox rubs elbows with an iconic photo of supermodel Kate Moss.*

OPPOSITE: *A round stool stands in for a nightstand—but can serve as extra seating when needed. Pieces by Tyler Mitchell, Karin Haas, and Emma Currie decorate an ever-changing gallery wall.*

When contemplating her 350-square-foot studio, Natasha refers to "the bigness of small," or the level of intention that living in a tiny home demands. "Because limitation necessitates innovation. In a way, that's what the 'bigness' is: It's the depth of small. It makes you dig deeper to be more creative, to make the space meet your way of living," she explains. When you don't have endless square footage to devote to storage and decor, you have to be deliberate about what you bring into your life, what you hold on to, what you display. On the one hand, this is a challenge, but on the other, you're more likely to find yourself surrounded by only what you love and find useful, as there is simply no room for the extraneous. In that way, these small-space lessons can be applied to abodes of any size.

Play with Scale

It seems logical that in a small home all the furniture should be similarly scaled, but tiny chairs, couches, and coffee tables can make the space feel unmoored without sturdier pieces to anchor the room. Instead, lean into your priorities to ground your design. Natasha prioritized entertaining, so she made room for a larger dining table than most would choose for a studio. If you value a comfortable gathering spot for family, opt for a spacious sectional; if clothing is a creative outlet for you, invest in an armoire that you'll use now and take with you to your next place. Don't be afraid to mix in one or two pieces that feel substantial. Oversize windows, art, mirrors, pendant lights, and rugs will always be welcome in any size space. Because these elements won't interfere with how you move through the room, they are a practical way to play with scale.

Let It Flow

When Lisa first moved into her studio, she arranged all the furniture, including her bed (page 73), up against the walls in an effort to eke out more livable space. She soon realized that the flow of the apartment didn't feel quite right—plus, it was more difficult to make the bed in the morning. In a very tiny space, lining the walls may be the only option, but where possible, try pulling your bed and sofa away from the walls to establish some breathing room.

OPPOSITE: *Visual dividers establish zones in a studio, without partitioning off an already small space. In Natasha's apartment, a walnut veneer bookcase separates the kitchen from the writing nook.*

GIACOMETTI YVES BONNEFOY

Rethink the Lighting

Especially in an urban apartment, bad lighting—scant natural sunlight and harsh overheads—is a common problem. To start, clean the windows to maximize the amount of sunlight that streams through them. Avoid blocking the windows with furniture or decor. If privacy is an issue, try a translucent window film or a sheer curtain that allows light to filter through. Take a cue from hotel rooms and choose a double curtain rod, which lets you layer both sheer and blackout curtains. Rather than illuminate a small space with light emitted from a single overhead source, which can feel harsh, arrange multiple light sources lower in the room, then let light bulbs that cast a soft, warm glow create a cozy atmosphere. Introduce a mix of table and floor lamps, wall-mounted sconces, and clip-on lamps. If you own your home, installing dimmer switches will let you set the tone for relaxing and entertaining. In a rental, opt for a plug-in lamp dimmer (available online or at hardware stores)—by plugging the lamp into the dimmer and then plugging the dimmer into an outlet, you can transform any floor or table lamp into a dimmable lamp. Just be sure you're using LED bulbs labeled "dimmable" to prevent strobing. And to adjust the brightness of a ceiling light or pendant light without rewiring, invest in a dimmable smart switch or screw in a smart light bulb that you can control from your phone.

Add Mirrors

When using mirrors to bounce sunlight around a room, placement is key. Setting a mirror across from a window will not only reflect sunlight, but a quick glance in the mirror will also give the impression that there's another window in the room. Bars and restaurants employ this trick all the time—an entire wall of mirrors can even fool you into thinking another room lies beyond. Consider placing a mirror behind your kitchen sink if you don't have a window to look out of, or set a full-length mirror in an entryway with a glass front door to flood the foyer with sunlight.

Free Up Floor Space

OPPOSITE:

In Natasha's sleep space, a C-shaped table hugs the edge of the bed, providing a surface for a tap-on, tap-off lamp and whatever bedside reading is on deck. In lieu of an entryway, a soapstone bowl sits atop a tall stack of books, collecting keys and wallets.

Oftentimes, our floors are overflowing while our walls are blank slates. To maximize valuable floor space and make your home easier to navigate, lift your furniture and belongings up off the ground. Consider wall-mounted nightstands, floating shelves, and hanging pendant lights. Replace a standing coatrack with wall hooks in a small entryway, or let two sconces on either side of the bed stand in for a floor lamp in a tiny bedroom. In a rental, plug-in sconces and pendant lamps help you avoid hardwiring, while a C-shaped cigar table (like the one beside Natasha's bed, pictured opposite) can wrap around the edge of a bed or sofa and doesn't require drilling holes in the wall. Furniture lofted on legs, whether sofas or dressers, show more of the floor, help the room look less cluttered, and make cleaning easier.

Accentuate the Room's Assets

If you're lucky enough to have any interesting architectural details in your home, show them off. Have a huge paned window in your little loft? Paint the window frame in a contrasting color (or line it in electrical tape, renters) to draw attention to the view. Blessed with high ceilings? Position a curtain rod close to the ceiling or crown molding so the curtain flows all the way down to the floor, accentuating the height of the space. Archways, fireplaces, and staircases all call for a little extra attention, too.

Do a Disappearing Act

To prevent visual clutter, allow some pieces to fade into the background. In Lisa's apartment, items that are necessary but not necessarily attractive—an air purifier, a humidifier, storage cabinets—were bought in white so they could blend into the walls. Similarly, transparent furniture, such as a clear acrylic desk or a glass side table, serves its purpose without stealing the show.

Embrace Temporary Solutions

When you're working with very limited square footage, the same square foot has to serve several purposes. If you're tight on kitchen counter space, measure your kitchen sink and get a cutting board that will fit across the top. Rest the cutting board over the sink as you meal prep, then wash it and stow it away when it's time to do the dishes. Movable furniture—like a wall-mounted desk that folds away at the end of the workday or a bar cart that will roll in at happy hour—helps the space adapt. If you entertain often, invest in a set of folding or stacking chairs to give each guest a seat; when the party's over, the chairs nest together to save space.

Prioritize Multifunctional Furniture

Particularly if you've lived in several homes, it's easy to accrue furniture and decor that doesn't fit your current space or your evolving aesthetic. Pare down what you keep, making space for flexible, multipurpose pieces—a table for both dinner parties and paint projects, a sofa that folds out into a bed for guests. Sell or give away unwanted items on Craigslist, Facebook Marketplace, or AptDeco to save furniture from the landfill.

OPPOSITE: *The secret to a cohesive-looking studio? Everything in Lisa's apartment, including the original painting by Carly Wilhelm, follows the color palette of the skate decks above the bed.*

Try a Quick Fix

When you want a little (almost) instant gratification, focus in on one room that feels cramped or cramps your style. Here's how to revamp it in the least amount of time, for the least amount of money. Cue the make-over scene.

Ten minutes: Improve the lighting. Turn off the overheads and switch on a couple of light fixtures set lower down in the room—table lamps, floor lamps, and sconces all count. If

you don't have enough secondary lighting in the room, shop the rest of your home for lamps to borrow. When illuminated with soft, ambient light, the space (and everything in it) will instantly look better.

Two hours: Fix the flow. Enlist the help of a furniture-moving friend or partner, then reevaluate the room's layout. If the back of your sofa is snug against the wall, try pulling it 12 inches into the room. If your bed is currently stuck in a corner of the bedroom, try repositioning it so the headboard is against a wall and there is space on both sides. Play with arrangements until the room is easy to navigate and each piece has some breathing room.

An afternoon: Paint! Brushing on a coat of paint is one of the fastest, most affordable ways to transform a room. Select the most space-expanding color based on the available light. In a small, sun-drenched room, white (warm white in a north-facing space; cool white in a south-facing space) creates a feeling of openness. In a dim interior room with little to no natural light, soft black or navy paint will lend depth, casting the corners into shadow so the limits of the room recede. Just make sure the hue matches the mood. Sumptuous and romantic, dark paint makes for an atmospheric dining room or bedroom but may make you feel drowsy in a home office.

Chapter 4
SHARED

three
times the
charm

JULIA STEVENS, PARIS FABRIKANT, AND TORI JENNER

- Williamsburg, Brooklyn
- 800 Square Feet
- Rented

"Tori is tech support, Paris is resident DJ, and I'm housekeeper," Julia Stevens says. "I'll wake up and she'll be Swiffering every single morning," Paris Fabrikant affirms. The three roommates first met through a mutual friend and moved into a sun-starved apartment in the Bushwick neighborhood of Brooklyn. Just two weeks after Tori Jenner moved in, they became fast friends when Paris developed a migraine, prompting a trip to the local hospital. "You know how people bond in a moment of crisis?" Julia asks. The bond was so strong that after two years in their first apartment, they decided to decamp together to a bigger, brighter loft in Williamsburg.

"It was by chance that we ended up moving," Paris says. Julia spotted a four-bedroom on StreetEasy for the same price as their three-bedroom, so she emailed it to the group. That particular apartment didn't end up working out. "But then you get the bug, and you want to keep looking," Julia explains. "And sometimes, you just want something exciting to happen in your life. There's nothing more exciting than moving," she says. "And stressful," Tori counters. "It's exciting in theory, and then you actually have to do it, and you're like, 'Wow,'" Paris settles it. That's how the conversation flows with these three: They're quick to finish each other's sentences, cut in with their own version of the story, or pepper in some missing details.

The new apartment was ideal in most ways–huge windows (even in the bathroom!), an open layout living area, surprisingly well-chosen fixtures–but the deal almost fell through because of one major deficit: storage space. The building offered to construct closets in their bedrooms, but with each room measuring roughly 8 x 12 feet, they didn't have much square footage to spare. Instead, the roommates decided to convert one side of the apartment's wide hallway into a communal closet.

At first, they bounced around the idea of closed wardrobes, but they ended up opting for a more economical open closet crafted from $6 rods and plywood procured from a local lumberyard. The total project cost: less than $150. All three were pleased–that is, until the clothing rods ripped out of the wall and came crashing down. "I heard it in the middle of the night and was so horrified," Paris says. The next day, they bought the right wall anchors, and the closet has been securely attached ever since. To make sharing the closet easier, the columns act as dividers, indicating where one roommate's section ends and another's begins. "I think dividing up the space and knowing what your territory is, is the key to sharing." Julia says.

embrace your space

OPPOSITE: *(From left) Tori, Paris, and Julia in their dining area.*

ABOVE: *Paris's dad may (or may not) have pilfered the silver tissue box from a now-defunct hotel when he was a teenager.*

OPPOSITE: *The roommates repurposed the wooden shelving from their previous apartment but added two more shelves to take full advantage of the loft's soaring ceilings. Interspersed among the art books are pieces with storied pasts. Julia unearthed the bust that serves as the centerpiece of the display at Santa Monica Airport's antiques market and lugged it home in a tote bag. The green urn above belonged to Paris's grandmother. Two cow figurines are a nod to Paris's family's country home, which friends affectionately call the "Cow House," thanks to her parents' collection of cow-themed memorabilia. "There's a life-size cow statue in their backyard," Julia says. "He's named Milky Way; I named him in the sixth grade," Paris adds.*

Some shared design sensibilities also help feather a harmonious nest. It certainly doesn't hurt that all three work in the design world: Tori is a fashion design assistant studying at the Fashion Institute of Technology; Paris is an interior design consultant studying at Pratt; and Julia is a style editor at *Domino*. Collectively, they swear by a mix of old and new, and they eschew anything too trendy. Much of the furniture in the loft—including the velvet sofa and the pony hair-upholstered Alky chair by Giancarlo Piretti—was sourced from Paris's dad, a fashion designer with a degree in architecture and an affinity for vintage home furnishings. "A lot of the furniture is special, because I grew up with it," Paris says.

The main living area adheres to a fairly neutral color palette while the bedrooms provide a space to play with color and pattern and showcase personal interests and collections. To establish a sense of continuity throughout the apartment, each bedroom features the same white curtains from Pottery Barn. "With roommates, each room is each person's own decisions, but to pick something that feels more permanent, such as curtains, and have it all the same in each room makes it feel more like a family designed the whole house," Julia explains. Tori nods in agreement: "It feels more like a home. More like one collective home."

OPPOSITE: *After realizing that the very limited drawer space in their kitchen wasn't going to cut it, Julia, Paris, and Tori took a page from Julia Child's playbook and hung a pegboard on the wall to hold tongs, strainers, and cheese graters. By paying attention to pain points in the apartment, the roommates came up with inventive ways to help their household run more smoothly. "Everything we did was a solution to a problem. And the problem is usually that there's no storage," Julia says.*

This communal approach extends beyond decor, to food—when someone cooks dinner, they make enough for the whole house—and even pets—Tori and Paris are coparents to Jack, a seventy-pound hound with heart-meltingly sad eyes. While fostering Jack, they soon fell in love with him and stopped answering calls from other hopeful pet parents. (Appropriately,

Jack landed a spot as the cover model on an issue of *New York* magazine when they ran a feature on the highly competitive market for rescue dogs.) Now, Paris and Tori share the responsibility of caring for Jack—a lifelong commitment they commemorated with matching stick-and-poke tattoos of Jack's name—but they both know that they won't live together forever.

"We have such a special friendship, I feel like we'll be able to work it out. We don't plan on leaving New York anytime soon," Paris says. "Both of our schedules are so busy, it will be nice to have a flow, an excuse to see each other and have some quality time." Their status as roommates may be temporary, but as friends, well, that's forever.

a

well-feathered

nest

LINDSAY AND ROB MACRAE

- ◆ Upper West Side, Manhattan
- ◆ 850 Square Feet
- ◆ Rented

After working on commercial projects for big architecture firms like Gensler and Robert A.M. Stern Architects for the better part of a decade, interior designer Lindsay MacRae took the leap into residential design in an unconventional manner: She asked a woman who was pregnant at her gym if she had a nursery designed for the baby yet. She did not. Lindsay offered to take on the project for free, in exchange for experience and photos of the finished space—Lindsay MacRae Interiors was born.

"I originally just wanted to do nurseries because they're just these happy spaces," she says. "And it's so exciting when there's a baby on the way." She quickly learned that keeping her fledgling design firm afloat would require branching out to other rooms in the house, yet nurseries never lost their glow. For years, Lindsay ran the business out of her home office, creating nurseries (and living rooms and bedrooms and kitchens) for clients buzzing with excitement over their growing families, yet she resigned herself to the idea that she may never have a child of her own—until the unexpected happened: She was pregnant.

Lindsay and her husband, Rob, eagerly cleared out their spare bedroom—previously stacked floor-to-ceiling with pillows and props for photo shoots and interior design projects—to make space. Then, while flipping through wallpapers at John Rosselli's showroom, Lindsay spotted it: Dorothy Draper's Les Fleurs de Toulon, a punchy floral pattern, and knew it was destined for her future child's room. "For me, working with pattern isn't scary. I think white walls are really scary," she says. "Once you get the pattern, it's so easy—everything will just fall into place. I feel like it's almost cheating; the work is done for you." To avoid competing with the riot of blooms on the walls, Lindsay chose voluminous white curtains, a white rug, and a white crib. The poppy-red slipper chair pulls in an accent color from the wall covering, and "it was literally the only chair that we could fit through the door," she says. To map out the narrow room, the designer drew it in a 3D modeling program, even planning a route for the chair to squeeze into the space, thanks to a series of lifts and swivels she first choreographed virtually and then relayed to the movers.

RIGHT: *A two-tier shelving unit tucks beside the pedestal sink—the top holds a candle and cotton swabs, while the lower level stocks toilet paper.*

OPPOSITE: *The bedroom mixes patterns—intricate florals on the throw pillow, stripes on the blanket, a ship motif on the bedding—all unified by a blue-and-white color palette. Similar to the wallpaper in Sloane's nursery, one pattern launched the entire design: The nautical Serena & Lily bedsheets guided the color scheme and the feeling of the space.*

Living in a rental, Lindsay decided to take a calculated risk and not ask the building owner's permission before hanging the wallpaper in the nursery because (1) she was so in love with the pattern that she couldn't bear the heartbreak of hearing no, and (2) she refused to repeat the mistakes of apartments past. In their previous rental, the couple delayed decorating, haunted by the nagging worry of "What's going to happen when we move?" After five years of living with white walls, Lindsay finally added bold stripes to the apartment's tiny vestibule. They moved five months later. "We should have just put this up from the very beginning and we could have enjoyed it," she remembers thinking. This time, the gamble paid off twofold: Lindsay not only got her security deposit back in full (she and Rob have since moved to Florida to be near family), but she also ended up designing what is still her "favorite space in the entire world." Once her daughter Sloane arrived, the nursery fulfilled its promise as a cherished place for both baby and parents. "I never wanted to leave that room. I was so happy there," Lindsay says.

Unfortunately, not every room in the apartment came together with such kismet. The living room presented the biggest design challenge. Serving as the entryway, the hangout zone, and the dining area, it had to compromise on all three fronts. To make up for not having a coat closet, Lindsay recruited a sturdy armoire (sourced from the kids' section at Restoration Hardware, where "you can get the same stuff, but it's a little bit smaller and less expensive," says Lindsay) to stash coats and shoes near the

front door. To fit the armoire, they had to forgo a dining table, so meals were eaten on two sofas set face to face. What the room lacked in layout, it made up for with beautiful furniture in durable, family-friendly materials. The black-and-white tweed sofa camouflaged the shedding fur of Pork Chop, the couple's Jack Russell terrier. Beneath the coffee table, a small antique area rug from ABC Carpet & Home proved indestructible, surviving spilled drinks without leaving any telltale stains.

The layout never stopped the couple from opening up their home to friends—but in the absence of a dining table, they traded sit-down dinners for intimate cocktail parties. Guests would mix up drinks at the bar cart before mingling on the sofas. If they got hungry, the place on the corner always had a table waiting for them.

OPPOSITE: *While residing on the Upper West Side, the armoire served as a coat closet, but in its new home in Florida, it acts as Sloane's (very elegant) toy chest. Invest in versatile, timeless furniture and it will live many lives as your family's needs change. The Mickey Mouse art above the Louis Ghost chair by Philippe Starck alludes to a bit of personal history: Lindsay and Rob first met while working at Disney World in their twenties.*

LEFT: *A brass bar cart, sourced from 1stdibs, inspired the couple's cocktail parties.*

The neighborhood helped fill in the gaps and made amends for the difficulties of apartment life. Each week, Rob (with Pork Chop in tow) would haul heavy bags of clothes and bedding to the laundromat a few blocks away, and construction in the unit upstairs once brought a sleepless-with-a-newborn Lindsay close to tears. But the city atoned for these frustrations with its singular magic. The bedroom windows provided a perfect vantage point from which to watch the Macy's Thanksgiving Day Parade balloons inflate the evening before the big event; in springtime, Lindsay would throw open the window in her office to let the sounds of a neighbor practicing the French horn flow in; in winter, flurries would fall on the back courtyard below, blanketing the city in soft, quiet snow. "It was so very New York."

TOP: *Behind Lindsay's desk, a burlap-wrapped bulletin board collects fabric swatches, birthday cards, and words of encouragement.*

ABOVE: *The vintage Thomasville dresser sorts tile and paint samples, while the top provides a place to lay out design plans and peruse wallpaper options.*

OPPOSITE: *A transparent console table stealthily squeezes another work surface into the room. The clear design doesn't demand much attention, allowing the Vitra Panton chair (Lindsay's college graduation present) to steal the show.*

When you live by yourself, you have the luxurious freedom to steer your own ship. You can decorate however you please (barring the restraints of budget or leasing contracts or HOA rules, of course). But when you share your space with a partner, kids, parents, or roommates, designing a home becomes a dialogue. It necessitates conversation and compromise, but this push and pull can make a space more dynamic than it would have been if designed from a singular perspective. When Lindsay moved in with her husband, Rob, she expected to have free rein over the decor choices because she is, after all, a professional designer. Turns out, he had his own opinions about how their space should feel and function. While some of his suggestions were brushed aside, others, like his choice of the leather settee in the living room (pictured right), stuck. At first, Lindsay protested that it didn't match the black-and-white tweed sofa already in the room, but she later conceded, "it kind of works in a weird way." In the end, the mix is far more interesting than a matching set.

OPPOSITE: *A gilded Louis Philippe mirror bounces light from the adjacent windows in Lindsay and Rob's living room.*

Start the Conversation

It's trite but true: Communication is at the heart of every relationship. This means listening to the needs of those you live with and expressing your needs in turn. With adults and older kids, start a conversation. Ask everyone to write down their top five priorities for their home—it could be a quiet spot to study, the freedom to have friends over, or the ability to paint their bedroom their favorite color. Everyone won't have all five met all the time, but if at all possible, work to ensure each person's top priority is honored.

Learning about what matters most to each person will help you understand where they're coming from, and keeping these priorities in mind could help avoid or defuse conflicts. If one roommate says they envision home as a space to entertain, and another says they want home to be a private retreat, a compromise over when guests are allowed, how many, and with how much advance notice could avoid future arguments. Continue the conversation, as each person's needs will change over time. Younger kids and pets won't be able to express themselves as directly, but they still communicate if you listen and observe. For example, Lindsay knew her dog, Pork Chop, would want his own spot in her home office so he could stay close to her as she worked. She topped the radiator in the room with an upholstered cushion to give Pork Chop the best seat in the house—with warmth, a view, and company. Pork Chop cherished his throne, and Lindsay still says it was one of her favorite details in the apartment.

Find Common Ground

If you can, try to find some commonality in your design styles. Make a shared Pinterest board with your partner or roommates, and start adding inspiration images of how you would each like the space to look. You can include furniture, paint swatches, rooms you'd like to emulate. Once you've all contributed some fodder, comb through the board for any similarities in style. Perhaps you both pinned different shades of blue paint, or you both gravitate toward homes with houseplants. Find the common threads and weave them through your shared space. And if there is no common ground? Stick to neutral ground. For the communal areas, choose neutral hues and functional furniture with simple shapes; save the peel-and-stick wallpaper and bright paint for your bedroom or your own separate space.

OPPOSITE: *Follow Lindsay and Rob's lead and decorate your home with shared memories. The black-and-white photo prints are of the beach in Rio de Janeiro, one of the couple's favorite cities.*

Choose Organizers That Fit Your Life

Organization helps everyone find what they need, preventing fights and unnecessary frustration. Rather than establish a system as soon as you move in, spend a couple of weeks simply observing how you all live in the new house or apartment. If you find that shoes tend to pile up near the front door, invest in a shoe rack, a wall-mounted cabinet, or a storage bench for the entryway. Instead of resisting the habit and insisting everyone return their shoes to their bedrooms (and inciting rebellion from tired children every time you get home), incorporate storage that works with, rather than against, your family's natural routines. Storage should fit your life—not the other way around.

Make It Easy to Clean

If you're sharing your space with kids, pets, or messy roommates, or if you are messy yourself, designing an easy-to-clean home will save you extra effort (and heartbreak) later. When picking out paint, keep in mind that shinier finishes wipe clean more quickly. For wall paint, opt for an eggshell finish—it's a higher sheen than matte or flat, but it won't look shiny. On molding and trim, choose semigloss so smudges and fingerprints will wipe away easily. When shopping for sofas, consider leather, which won't collect as much fur as woven upholstery, or look for performance fabrics in colors that will hide your pet's fur. Sofas and chairs with removable slipcovers that can be tossed in the washing machine will stand up to spills and dirty paw prints. Start with forgiving furniture that matches your household's mess level, and these pieces will last for years.

Carve Out Your Own Area (and Let Others Carve Out Theirs)

Take a cue from Julia, Paris, and Tori's loft: Let each roommate's bedroom (pictured opposite) reflect their own personal style. In a family, sectioning off your own space is equally as important. If square footage allows, it can be an entire room, but it doesn't have to be. In Aya's apartment, the lofted nook near the front door provides a place for her kids to play independently (page 118). Tucked behind a wall, the area feels private, yet the open design lets Aya check in on them. A closet that's had the door removed and replaced with a curtain can become a play space for a little one, while a bathroom that the kids don't use can turn into an oasis for adults. Brush a spare wall with chalkboard paint that your children are free to scribble and draw on as they wish, and consider an enclosed cat cave that your pet can retreat to when they want some alone time. Shared spaces require compromise in terms of noise levels, distractions, and activities, so it's helpful to have at least one area to decompress.

LEFT: *Paris describes her personal style as a "World of Interiors, rustic, mixed with some new chrome elements." Whether old or new, she prefers "something that has a story and a heart."*

BOTTOM LEFT: *Tori sneaks extra storage into her bedroom with slatted underbed bins, a simple dresser embellished with leather handles, and a sturdy wooden chest.*

BOTTOM RIGHT: *Braided hats, woven bags, and a cabana-striped duvet cover reflect Julia's West Coast roots. "That's sort of the California in me," she says.*

Split Your Space

When you have a small home with only so many rooms (or maybe your entire home is just one room), it's inevitable that some spaces will have to serve more than one function. Your home office might be buzzing all day, then when five o'clock strikes, the floor is cleared and the yoga mat rolls out. But when one room needs to serve several functions simultaneously, like a living room that's a home gym for you and a homework zone for the kids, that's where dividers come in. Determine whether you want a barrier that's temporary or permanent, then try one of these smart ways to separate a space.

Bookcase: A tall bookcase provides ample storage for your home library and serves as a brilliant room divider. Let a bookcase section off the sleeping area in a studio or a play zone for the kids in the living room. Choose from an open bookcase or a closed one, depending upon how much privacy you'd like to establish. To prevent the piece from toppling over, anchor one side to the wall using metal brackets and sturdy wood screws or the hardware supplied by the manufacturer.

Canopy bed: In a studio or a bedroom that doubles as a home office, a canopy bed—especially one draped with curtains—makes the bed feel like a private oasis.

Curtains: For any situation that calls for semiprivacy, like a kids' space that you want to keep an eye on, a curtain is the answer. And if you wish you could add just one more door or wall in your rental, grab a curtain. For a makeshift door, secure a cafe curtain rod (or a sturdy tension rod if you want to avoid drilling holes) across the doorway and hang up the curtain; for a makeshift wall to divide open living spaces, suspend diaphanous fabric from a track on the ceiling.

Folding panel room dividers: Sometimes, you just want a simple visual barrier—that's where a folding room divider comes in. Unfurl it when you want some privacy, then stow it away when you need extra space. From woven rattan designs to an undulating Eames molded plywood screen, there's an option to match every style.

Plants: Arrange large, leafy houseplants in elevated plant stands and trailing vines in hanging planters to create the illusion of privacy between areas of a bedroom or living room. Or set plants on top of a long, low storage cabinet to boost its height and act as a subtle screen.

OPPOSITE: *In Sloane's nursery, the design is a balance between Lindsay's polished style and baby-proof pieces. Lindsay splurged on the wallpaper, but saved on a soft, inexpensive rug, knowing that it would face many messes.*

Let Values Guide Your Layout

How you set up your home will influence how your family interacts—so choose a layout that aligns with your priorities. In Aya's apartment, the open kitchen (pictured right) encourages her kids to get involved in cooking (and did we mention, her twelve-year-old son actually does the dishes). In Lindsay's living room (page 101), the two sofas face each other rather than angle toward the TV, so the focus is on conversation and connection. Your home should help you live the life you want, so starting with a vision for your family's day-to-day life will demystify the design process.

OPPOSITE: *In Aya's kitchen, the priority for her is to have clean work areas, whether for cooking, doing homework, or crafts with her kids.*

Chapter 5
LUSH

urban oasis

AYA MACEDA AND KURT ARNOLD

- Cobble Hill, Brooklyn
- 750 Square Feet
- Owned

Whenever they would stroll around northwestern Brooklyn, architect Aya Maceda and her husband, photographer Kurt Arnold, would admire a particular building: a former ship provisions factory nestled into a block of brownstones. "We were always intrigued by this building that had these massive windows, and we would always think, 'How amazing would the light be in those apartments?'" Aya says. She decided to look up the building online—as luck would have it, a unit posted for sale that same day.

On a tour of the apartment, they quickly realized it didn't make any sense for a growing family "because it was basically a giant studio," Aya explains. But it was too late for practicality; the sunlight spilling in through the 8-foot-tall windows had already sold them. With Aya's design prowess—she's a cofounder of the architecture firm ALAO—the couple knew they could make the space work. She saw the vision immediately.

"Our priority was to have these big, open spaces for work and play for the family," Aya says. "We like to be together in one space; it's culturally in line with how we live. We're kind of all on top of each other, but then we have our own sleeping areas that don't need to be massive." Before moving in, they let go of half of their clothing, only holding on to what they really needed, and gave away the rest. To save money on renovations, they remodeled in phases synchronized with summer trips when the family planned to be away. The first phase entailed remodeling the kitchen and downstairs powder room, installing a desk beneath the stairs, and constructing a guest bed (with a lofted play space for the kids) near the front door. The second phase focused on the upstairs sleeping areas, including building a primary bedroom off the original sleeping loft. The room lacks an exterior window, but it borrows views of the tree-lined street below thanks to an interior window; sunlight is supplied by the new skylight above.

OPPOSITE: *All the covers on the white LC2 sofa are removable and washable, making it a more sustainable decor choice for a family with kids. "And then Woolite is my friend," Aya says. On the white walls, a Mr. Clean Magic Eraser is her go-to stain remover. "I'm very forgiving, too, with mess. It's just a part of life."*

Throughout the renovation, Aya held fast to two guiding principles. One: maaliwalas, a Filipino concept that means "a generous flow of light and air, this feeling of expansiveness that gives you well-being when you come into the space," Aya explains. And two: her childhood home, which exemplifies the concept. Growing up in the Philippines, she lived in an architect-designed courtyard house that didn't look anything like the other buildings in the neighborhood. To recreate the feeling of a courtyard, of life orbiting around plants, Aya placed a towering tree at the center of her Brooklyn apartment. When her daughter, Lulu, was learning how to walk, she would use the tree's sturdy planter to hoist herself up—and then nibble some soil from the pot. To prevent this, Aya asked a woodworker friend, Scott Raffaele, to help design a locking cover for the planter. Now that Lulu is six and has long outgrown this phase, the cover serves as a perch for books or a glass of water.

A sense of nostalgia steers both plant placement and plant choices throughout the loft. Every time Aya sees the fiddle leaf fig tree—its leaves reminiscent of the almond trees found in the Philippines—she thinks back on her childhood home. "It's the same with the philodendrons, and the monsteras, and the orchids," she says. "'What do I recall from my childhood?' is what we were searching for, and what we were recreating and putting into our own home." Kurt, who was born in Grenada and raised in Brooklyn, also has a fondness for tropical plants, and the philodendrons trailing from the upstairs balcony are reminders of the vines seen cascading from rock ledges around waterfalls in the Caribbean. In keeping with the tropical theme, their twelve-year-old son, Kosi, picked out the air plants. "We always go to plant stores together as a mom-and-son activity," Aya explains.

OPPOSITE: *A Yoda chair by Kenneth Cobonpue sits in front of an arrangement of Kurt's photography. In place of a television, the family uses a projector and a screen that rolls down in front of the gallery wall. They didn't want a TV to take up any wall space "just because our priority was to hang art," Aya says.*

LEFT: *Under the stairs, Kurt's desk area doubles as a gallery space for treasured artwork from Australia and the Philippines, along with travel keepsakes, an ant farm, and an orange golf ball commemorating a particularly impressive swing by Kosi.*

Aya was used to homegrown vegetables as a child, so when the COVID-19 pandemic hit New York City, sparking anxieties about food insecurity, she stepped up her humble herb garden into a miniature vegetable farm. "I thought, 'Let's figure out a way to grow food at home, and that still looks good, that still works aesthetically with our home.'" Now, a hydroponic system by Gardyn sits at the bottom of the stairs and keeps the family stocked with butterhead lettuce, kale, chard, tomatoes, and enough basil to sustain their frequent pesto dinners, which Lulu helps prepare by harvesting leaves and smashing garlic. "Because of the setup, my kids cook," Aya says. "Because it's happening in the center of the house, they're always participating."

As the kids get older and their interests grow—Kosi's anime books demand real estate on the bookshelf; Lulu's empire of tiny toys expands—the family's fears of inevitably running out of room have prompted them to tour townhouses "because this is what we think we need; this is what society tells us is our next step." Yet after each tour, they return home to their apartment, where they're greeted by the nurturing flow of warm sunlight and fresh, plant-purified air, and think, "But we love our place."

TOP: *When Lulu was born, Aya's mother came to help out with the baby for several weeks and slept in the guest bed near the front door. Above the bed is a lofted play space for the kids. Aya wanted her children to hang out in the communal area of the apartment, but "I didn't want our apartment to be inundated with toys," she says. To balance both goals, she designed a nook that provides the kids with a sense of privacy yet makes it easy to keep an eye on them.*

ABOVE: *A hanging spider plant and an embroidered Otomi coverlet—Kurt's present to Aya during her fortieth birthday trip to Mexico—brighten up the bedroom.*

OPPOSITE: *While living in Australia for several years prior to New York, Aya worked with architect Alex Popov. Naja Utzon Popov, Alex's daughter, custom-made the rug in the kids' room to match the fur of Aya's old dog.*

Unhurried mornings with time for shared breakfast are a luxury that's not afforded by chance but rather built by design ... the trade-off of having a smaller home is the convenience of location.

To prolong the amount of time they can survive in just under 750 square feet, they have established a daily routine for tidying up. At night, Kosi and Kurt do a light cleaning. In the morning, Aya starts her day with a ritual offering to her family: She wakes up early to open the window shades, clear off the work surfaces, and cook breakfast, for which the family sits down and eats together before work and school. Unhurried mornings with time for shared breakfast are a luxury that's not afforded by chance but rather built by design. They could find a bigger place within their budget in another neighborhood, but the trade-off of having a smaller home is the convenience of location: Everything they need, including the kids' schools and plentiful food options, are nearby, "so we're able to have more time, because the radius of our day-to-day life is very small," says Aya. In exchange for living with less, they have gained the immeasurable gifts of time and togetherness.

OPPOSITE: *The painting by Angelito Antonio originally hung above Aya's childhood dining table in Manila. "It's very humid in the Philippines, so any works of art, after a few years, they start deteriorating," Aya says, explaining how her mother began giving away pieces of her art collection the year before her passing. The painting, gifted to Kosi, depicts women harvesting tobacco leaves.*

garden
apartment

KAYLYN HEWITT

- Santa Monica, California
- 700 Square Feet
- Rented

Six days before her one-way flight from Boston to Los Angeles, Kaylyn Hewitt had no clue where she was going to live. Having accepted a job as the lead floral designer at the Bouqs Company, she was about to move her entire life cross-country, yet she had only been to LA a handful of times and had only the vaguest understanding of the city's numerous sprawling neighborhoods. "I was like, 'I guess I'm going to stay in a hotel when I get there.' We were in the eleventh hour," she says. But just days before hopping the flight, she spotted the rental listing: a sun-dappled bungalow in Santa Monica with a small back patio that was full of potential. The pieces fell into place.

The property owner took her on a video tour, and when Kaylyn mentioned Bear, her sixty-pound Labrador mix, he assured her, "No worries, we can deal with that." She signed the lease without ever stepping foot in the apartment. "I remember walking in . . . and just being like, 'This feels like my home. This was a necessity, I just had to go with it, but I actually think this has the bones to be a place where I can really, really thrive.'" To her delight, she soon discovered she had by luck landed in a quiet, walkable pocket of Santa Monica, which she says "feels like a small town in LA," a place where neighbors wave and chat as they walk their dogs at the same time every morning. A place where if you're waiting around, laden with photography gear on the tree-lined sidewalk, friendly locals will wonder what you're working on and offer for you to take a peek inside their homes when they hear it's a decor book. Where a mail carrier will walk by, and everyone will stop to greet each other by name.

ABOVE: *Woven elements—the pendant lamp, the rattan chair from Urban Outfitters, and the bamboo doors on the Ivar cabinet in the dining room—infuse Kaylyn's home with a beachy, bohemian sense of ease. By staying true to what she loves, the result is a space that feels like her, and the aesthetic runs through all facets of her life.*

OPPOSITE: *Container gardens are ideal for temporary living spaces. Kaylyn can enjoy the fragrant lavender and beautiful mandevilla blooms now, then transport them to the next place whenever she moves. The same principle applies to the string lights suspended overhead and the outdoor table from World Market.*

Finding the bungalow follows a repeating pattern in Kaylyn's life: pieces suddenly falling into place. After studying psychology and child development at Baylor University in Waco, Texas, she signed up for a master's program in Boston with the goal of becoming a child life specialist. That summer, several of Kaylyn's friends asked her to arrange the flowers for their weddings. "I've always been the DIY, creative friend," she explains. Over the span of eighteen months, she went from never having considered a career in floral design to realizing what she calls her "true vocation" as a florist and launching her own company, True Vine Studio.

In retrospect, it shouldn't have come as such a surprise. Kaylyn grew up with a rambling, English-style garden that her parents cultivated at their home outside of Dallas. When she was dropped off at college, while other parents were imploring their kids to study or reminding them to floss, she will never forget her mom's send-off: "Make sure you always have fresh flowers." Looking back, she can see the path that led her to floral design, but "in the moment, it was this puzzle coming together that I didn't even know was coming together," she says.

As a housewarming present, her mom gifted her two large potted bougainvillea plants, which grow wild all over LA and whose pink-to-orange petals reflect the color palette woven throughout the apartment. At first, she planned to decorate entirely with warm whites and sunset hues, until practicality prohibited a white sofa and led her instead to a gray West Elm sectional that could hide pet fur while providing plenty of seating for friends. Her home couldn't feel too precious, she notes: "A dog lives there, flower petals are typically all over the place." To ensure the blend of cool and warm tones would work, Kaylyn first laid everything out on a Pinterest board, starting with a throw pillow containing the blush and burnt orange hues she loves. Inspiration images sat beside credenzas and side tables she hoped to buy, and the selection was honed until every piece harmonized.

OPPOSITE: *An art print of wilting ranunculus from Juniper Print Shop coordinates with the bungalow's marigold-and-rose color palette, while illustrating the florist's fascination with the complete life cycle of plants. Kaylyn collects dried botanicals, like the palm fronds and eucalyptus on her dining table, and she has begun experimenting with drying the flowers grown on her patio. Plus, in Santa Monica, nature presents its own gifts. "There's tons of stuff that just falls off the trees," she says. "Bougainvillea is one that dries so beautifully."*

To stay on budget, Kaylyn embraced a fairly slow design process for a rental, which stretched out over the course of a year. She waited for big-ticket items, such as her ivory upholstered bed frame, to go on sale, and she scrolled resale sites in hopes of securing secondhand versions of the furniture she had pinned. Patience paid off, and she even scored her favorite piece, the vintage coffee table in her living room, while scrolling through an online marketplace.

Living on her own for the first time, Kaylyn finally had an opportunity to decorate a space that was a true reflection of herself. "This is my Miss Honey season," she says, referring to the fairytale cottage in the film adaptation of Roald Dahl's *Matilda*, "where I can have this cute little space, and it can just be completely me and my own." With dreams to replicate Miss Honey's garden, Kaylyn has sprinkled more than a dozen wildflower seed packets into the raised planters and window boxes lining her patio, along with some focal flowers, such as foxgloves. Two years in, the garden is another lesson in patience. She spent the first year learning how to grow blooms from seed and the second year observing what did and didn't thrive in the available sunlight. "It was just the journey of a gardener, which I think can be a really therapeutic thing on a lot of levels."

Following the big move from New England, Kaylyn also finds herself blooming in this space, nurtured by the warm, sunny climate and the close-knit community. Hoping to buy a house in the next couple of years, she would happily stay in the neighborhood if she can find a place within her budget. "I feel like I'm getting rooted here," she says.

ABOVE: *By mixing preserved plants (palm fronds) and live plants (a rubber tree and monstera), Kaylyn's apartment has a lush look—with half the maintenance.*

OPPOSITE TOP: *Brass knobs and drawer handles replaced the original hardware, adorning the cabinets like jewelry. By decanting pantry supplies—flour, oats, shredded coconut, dried rose petals—Kaylyn saves space previously devoted to bulky packaging and can spot when items are running low.*

OPPOSITE BOTTOM: *A leafy aglaonema helps clear the air in the bedroom; the chunky knit throw is from Bearaby.*

embrace your space

Plants contribute so much to the look and feel of our homes, but it's important to remember that they aren't just decorative elements—they're living things. Perhaps the best way to help a plant thrive is to familiarize yourself with its natural habitat, whether that's a rainforest or the desert. When caring for her towering bird-of-paradise (pictured opposite), Kaylyn says the key is "tricking it into thinking it's outside" by keeping the soil moist and placing it in the sunniest spot in the house. Considering your plants' preferred humidity levels, soil, and sun requirements will help them flourish inside your home.

Indoor Plants

Houseplants help a home come alive. Start with just one, then add as many as your square footage (and schedule) will allow.

Pick the Right Varieties

When choosing plants, visualize a Venn diagram: One side contains plants that match your desired aesthetic, and the other side consists of plants that will thrive in your home. Select plants at the intersection of these two categories. The first part is easy—search online, populate a Pinterest board, or visit a nursery to determine which plants you like the look of. Next, consider your home and lifestyle. How much sun does each room in your house get? Will you water the plant regularly, or is it likely you'll skip a watering or two (be honest!)? Introducing a new plant isn't just about where it will look best. It's also about where it will receive the conditions it needs. Some elements can be cheated indoors, like misting a plant to increase the moisture levels. If sunlight is an issue, choose low-light plant varieties or invest in grow lights.

Try Hydroponics

If you'd prefer to skip the soil (and bugs) or you tend to under- or overwater, grow your plants hydroponically. In Aya's apartment (pictured below), she grows greens and vegetables in a vertical hydroponic garden that requires just 2 square feet of floor space. Water from the reservoir at the bottom gets pumped up to the plants on a schedule while the LED light bars would provide enough light even if Aya's apartment didn't have those glorious windows. To test out hydroponics for less than $25, order an herb kit that works by passive hydroponics (no pumps or motors); an absorbent wick draws water up from a reservoir to the plant's roots. The beauty of this system: As long as you keep the reservoir filled with water, you can't accidentally under- or overwater.

OPPOSITE: *An arrangement of plants—including a soaring bird-of-paradise—demarcates Kaylyn's living room.*

LEFT: *Aya, Kurt, and their kids follow a pescatarian diet; the hydroponic garden at the foot of the stairs supplies them with herbs and vegetables.*

Listen to Your Plants

Rather than adhere to a strict watering schedule, check if the plant is thirsty by sticking your finger a couple of inches into the soil. The top layer of soil will dry out quickly, so testing below the surface level is a more accurate gauge. Depending upon seasonal shifts in your home's humidity levels, and whether or not the plant goes dormant in the winter, your houseplant may need varying levels of water throughout the year—this hands-on approach helps you adjust to your plant's current needs. Also look for yellow leaves, an important sign of distress that can be baffling to decode. Depending upon the plant variety, it could mean too much or too little water; check the soil moisture levels. Wilting is a similarly confusing symptom—again, it could indicate underwatering (the leaves droop without moisture) or overwatering (it could be the result of root rot). Test the soil and consider the humidity levels in your home.

Decorate with Houseplants

In a small space, a tall indoor tree delivers the drama. Choose a variety that doesn't grow too wide, so it will fill underutilized vertical space without blocking the flow of the room. To emphasize the height of your ceilings and draw the eye upward, set trailing plants on a high shelf or on top of your kitchen cabinets. When selecting plants, consider the texture (think, asparagus fern), color (like coleus), shape (hello, monstera), and even pattern (check out the polka-dot begonia).

ABOVE: *In this corner of David's bedroom, a trailing pothos suspended from the ceiling and a spiky dracaena set in an elevated planter lend visual interest at varying heights.*

Pot an Herb Garden

If you have a windowsill, you have room for an herb garden. Visit your local nursery for herbs, selecting those you tend to cook with most often, whether that's basil, rosemary, thyme, or chives. When you get home, transplant the herbs into pots with drainage holes, using a good-quality potting mix. Once potted, water each plant. Since most herbs thrive in full sun, line the herbs along a windowsill.

Low-Maintenance Houseplants

Aloe[1]*: This succulent originated in hot, arid desert climates and has long been used to soothe and heal burns. Find this plant a bright, sunny spot, then dial down the watering schedule to once every two to three weeks.

Boston fern[1]: In nature, ferns are generally found on the shaded forest floor, so it makes sense they can survive a low-light location (although they'll be happiest with sunlight filtered through a sheer curtain, mimicking dappled light through a leafy canopy). Keep the soil moist and mist this fern frequently.

Parlor palm[1]: This tall, leafy plant does well in moderate to bright indirect light, but it can survive in low light. Water every one to two weeks, allowing the soil to dry out in between.

Pothos[1]*: Set this trailing plant on a mantel, or hang it near a window so its heart-shaped leaves act as a curtain. Pothos will thrive and grow more quickly in bright, indirect light, but it can also tolerate low light and infrequent watering.

Snake plant[1]*: Since it grows up, not out, this variegated plant was made for small spaces. It will survive a skipped watering or two, but it doesn't do well with overwatering (it can develop root rot). Bright indirect light is best, but moderate to low light will work.

Spider plant[1]: A profusion of long, slender leaves with light-yellow and lime-green stripes give this plant its personality. Pot it in well-drained soil (allow it to dry out between waterings), and place it in a spot with moderate to bright indirect light. Watch for spider plant babies—offshoots of the parent plant—which can be propagated. Spiderettes make great gifts for friends who stop by.

ZZ plant[1]*: Very drought tolerant (you definitely want to let the soil dry out between waterings), this tropical plant with glossy leaves prefers lots of indirect light, but it's revered for its ability to survive even in an office with fluorescent lights.

[1]*Low-light plants: While many houseplants do best in bright indirect light, these varieties will tolerate living in the shadows. Keep in mind that plants kept in dim lighting may grow more slowly, have less variegated leaves, or fail to flower.*

* Toxic to cats and dogs: If you have pets who might nibble your houseplants, skip these varieties, which are toxic to both cats and dogs, according to the ASPCA.

Outdoor Plants

If you have a balcony or backyard, bring on the outdoor plants. For the easiest-to-care-for options, check your planting zone and choose native varieties.

Grow a Container Garden

For a low-maintenance garden you can reconfigure over time—and even take with you if you move—a container garden is the way to go. Rather than grow plants directly in the ground, select a mix of pots and planters for your deck, porch, patio, or balcony. Urns, plant stands, and rolling plant caddies can help vary the plant heights. A pot equipped with a support, whether a trellis or plant pole, gives vining plants a chance to climb. Here's how to pot an outdoor plant.

1. Check that the pot has a drainage hole in the bottom. Place a shard of broken terra-cotta from an old pot over the hole—it will keep the soil in the pot, while still allowing water to drain.
2. Add a layer of gravel to help with drainage.
3. Top with enough potting mix so that when you add the plant it will sit at the correct height.
4. Remove the plant from its nursery grow pot and gently loosen the roots (this is particularly important if the plant is root-bound, which means it has outgrown its pot and its roots are tangled together).
5. Gently place the plant in the pot, holding it upright with one hand as you fill in around the plant with potting mix, making sure to distribute it evenly so the plant is centered.
6. Even off the soil at the top, leaving about 1 to 2 inches between the top of the soil and the top edge of the pot.
7. Water the plant and let it adjust to its new home.

Potted plants tend to dry out more quickly than ones in in-ground gardens, so be prepared to water them often—up to every day in the summer. Container gardens make up for this extra effort with other benefits: There will be less weeds to pull, and if you realize a plant needs more or less sunlight, simply move the pot to another area of the deck or patio.

Know Your Zone

Before falling in love with specific plants, learn which planting zone you live in. Look up the USDA Plant Hardiness Zone Map—enter your zip code and it will provide your planting zone number, from 1 to 13. From now on, when choosing outdoor plants, check the plant tag to make sure it can survive in your zone. There are some ways to work around this (such as bringing perennials indoors in the winter), but for an easy-to-maintain garden, stay in your zone.

OPPOSITE: *On the deck David built with his dad, everything can be reconfirgured as needed: the modular seating, the lightweight tables, and the potted ferns in plant stands.*

Choose Native Varieties

Similarly, native plants, or those that originated in the area and can thrive without human intervention, will be the easiest to care for. They tend to require less water, pest control, and maintenance than other plants. Plus, they support the local wildlife, like bees, birds, and butterflies. The National Audubon Society and the National Wildlife Federation both have free online databases of native plants based on zip code.

Chapter 6
COLORFUL

an
Old-World
abode

MATTHEW DEROSIER AND CASEY GORRELL

- Ditmas Park, Brooklyn
- 900 Square Feet
- Owned

For Matthew DeRosier, decorating the one-bedroom he shares with his partner, Casey Gorrell, was the home-decorating equivalent of dyeing your hair following a breakup. After parting ways with an architecture firm that leaned into sleek, futuristic designs, Matthew sought "the complete opposite." Rather than reach for the hair dye, he picked up a gallon of jewel-toned paint. "It was springtime, and I was listening to Taylor Swift and just crying and painting the blue," he recalls, motioning to the central anteroom swathed in Hale Navy by Benjamin Moore. "It was therapeutic." The work breakup set in motion an exploration of color and texture that rippled room by room throughout the apartment.

The transformation didn't happen overnight, but the couple brushed on layers of color slowly over time, living with each addition to make sure it felt right. They painted the wall behind the sofa Tarrytown Green by Benjamin Moore, sat with it for six months, and then painted the wall with the windows one Friday night. For now, they've left the adjoining wall white to help brighten the space, although the plan is to one day hang textured wallpaper.

Reminiscent of a Parisian cafe with its marble-topped bistro table—a fortuitous Craigslist find—the kitchen dining nook's evolution also unfolded with deliberate slowness. Matthew hand-stenciled the pineapple pattern on the back wall over the course of several hours, including short breaks to rinse off the stencil and slightly longer ones to pause from the tedium of the task. ("I just don't have the attention span, to be completely honest. I get bored very easily," he admits.) Six months later, they had a chair rail wrapped around the room. In the spring of the following year, they installed scalloped molding wall panels from Home Depot. The outcome of these layered projects is a petite dining area infused with European flair, where they eat dinner together every night and decompress at the end of a long week with drinks and a few rounds of cribbage or backgammon.

LEFT: *After installing new marble countertops, the couple turned the leftover stone into three open shelves. On the adjacent wall, a magnetic knife rack and a metal rail holding kitchen tools max out the wall storage. Items deemed worthy of prime counter space have proven to be both attractive and functional: an antique coffee grinder and a Swedish cast-iron kitchen scale.*

OPPOSITE: *The sitting area is a study in contrast. Shades of white—the milk glass sconce, the upholstered sofa, and the opposing wall reflected in the mirror—pop against the pine green backdrop. The clean lines of the coffee table balance the romantic, curved edges of the settee.*

While Matthew says that the kitchen tends to be his domain, the decorating process for that room (and all others) was a compromise. "Being aware of everyone's needs and making it fit into this aesthetic—compromising, that's a huge part for me," he explains. He consulted with Casey on design decisions along the way, and even Cordelia, the couple's cat, was factored in. A fan of prowling on top of the kitchen cabinets, Cordelia was allowed to claim her own territory in the kitchen (even after she knocked a jar off the ledge). And when Casey needed

a space to work from home and play video games, they compromised on a slim steel desk from Room & Board, a modern departure from the home's period charm.

Vintage and preowned pieces sourced via Craigslist and AptDeco instill the apartment with a sense of history—and the acquisition of each one adds a chapter to the home's story. When they picked up the dining table, which belonged to its previous owner's grandfather, they first had to eradicate the spider nests harbored inside the table's hollow interior. "That was probably

ABOVE: *The pouf in the living room is a lounge for the couple's cat, Cordelia, but she'll happily curl up on any chair, lap, or antique rug she can find.*

OPPOSITE: *Casey and Matthew met while studying abroad, when Casey's program, located outside Rome, took a trip up to Florence, where Matthew's school was based. While on a return anniversary trip to Italy, they spotted the barrister bookcase they'd been searching for on eBay. The day they flew home to New York, they picked up a rental car, drove straight to Connecticut, and brought back the bookcase. Situated in a corner, it serves as a display case for candlesticks and salt and pepper shakers.*

the grossest piece we've brought back," Matthew says. The Fischel dining chairs arrived from Nevada aboard a Greyhound bus; they got lost along the way, extending their journey by a few weeks.

Although the apartment, clocking in around 900 square feet, is small by most standards, it's nearly double the size of the couple's previous Brooklyn rental. After realizing that the monthly rent for a two-bedroom was comparable to the monthly mortgage and maintenance for a one-bedroom in the area, they decided to buy. "When we got a bigger apartment, we were like, 'Okay, let's get more stuff,'" Casey says. They soon reevaluated. Over the next two years, they prioritized what they wanted to make space for—most notably a bar area for Casey, an amateur mixologist—and pared back the rest, including the media console formerly stationed below the TV, filled with items they never reached for. "We try to be very intentional about the pieces; it should be serving a function. If they're not, if they're just going to be storing stuff we don't use, why do you need it?" he asks.

The restrictions of a smaller home have been a catalyst for self-expression rather than a deterrent, prompting the pair to home in on an aesthetic and focus on what they really need to live the life they envision.

After years of thoughtful curation, the belongings that did make the cut reflect the couple's interests and hobbies. Inside the storage chest in the living room, an assortment of horns collected from Matthew's favorite store in Paris lie beside Farrow & Ball color fans and spare bud vases. A modular storage system maximizes space in the closet, where one shelf is devoted to vintage editions of Sorry! and Parcheesi from the 1970s. A storage locker in the basement of their building stows DIY supplies, including the brad nailer bought to secure decorative molding to the walls. The restrictions of a smaller home have been a catalyst for self-expression rather than a deterrent, prompting the pair to home in on an aesthetic and focus on what they really need to live the life they envision.

Now, as Matthew and Casey pour themselves into an upstate house they recently bought and are in the process of renovating, they're considering downsizing their city dwelling sometime in the not-too-immediate future. "We don't need as much room after being together for so long, understanding how we work together and what we need to survive," Matthew explains. Funneled through the constraints of space and budget, the couple has successfully distilled the essence of home.

embrace your space

OPPOSITE: *A few simple upgrades breathe new life into the bathroom. A shelving unit from Pottery Barn doubles the room's storage; a porcelain and milk glass sconce diffuses light. For an instant improvement, tie a bundle of eucalyptus to the curtain rod—the steam from the shower will waft the leaves' uplifting scent around the room.*

the house that *music* made

DAVID QUARLES IV

- Memphis, Tennessee
- 1,150 Square Feet
- Owned

In David Quarles IV's Memphis home, every room sings because each one started as a song. "For the den, it's Diana Ross, 'It's My House,'" he says, referring to the sun-soaked room you step into from the front door. "When I close my eyes and listen to it, and when I'm going through a song . . . it's kind of like I'm traveling in a portal of color." A synesthete, David associates music (and numbers) with colors—a power that sometimes caused confusion during his childhood (especially in math class), but that has served him well as a designer, both of jewelry and of interiors. By closing his eyes, listening to a song on repeat, and allowing the related waves of color to wash over him, David can translate music and feeling into concrete design elements: the paint color on the walls, the wood tones of the furniture, the way sunlight streams in through the windows. If he's collaborating with a client—like the redesign he recently completed for local tapas restaurant Pantà—he asks them for a playlist that conveys the desired mood for the space, then he listens to the songs again and again as a guide for his design.

OPPOSITE: *"It has to be local or remind me of a story that I love," David says about the artwork he collects. Both paintings on the back wall in the den are by local artists: Kea Woods on the left and Frances Berry on the right. David first met Frances at a Memphis arts festival, where she was painting portraits while on roller skates.*

This process can be a balm (or at least an effective distraction) during difficult life moments, like when his father was in the hospital and David painted the energetic mural in the dining room (page 155) in under two and a half hours, each brushstroke coordinated with the rhythm of bossa nova music. Fortunately, David's father is doing well, even rolling up on his motorcycle the day of our photo shoot and inviting us to see his band perform on Beale Street later that evening. It's no mystery where David's creative talents flow from—as a kid, he would assist his dad every weekend on DIY projects (while his mom ran "quality control," double-checking measurements), and he continues to call on his father whenever design plans, such as the deck outside, require carpentry.

When David first moved into the house in 2016, he didn't immediately start painting murals and constructing decks. Unintentionally gray carpeting and an artificial turf-lined sunroom meant there was plenty to be done, but David, who was feeling stifled in a corporate job at the time, lacked inspiration. "I didn't have any room to flex my creative muscle; I was just excited to have a house," he says.

Two years later, he left his desk job to take an interior design position at Stock & Belle, a local clothing and home decor shop. He started leasing out his house to tenants and moved into a rental loft in downtown Memphis so he could be closer to the shop. The blank slate of the rental, coupled with the energy of the new job, provided space for David to experiment with and hone his personal sense of style.

OPPOSITE: *David acquired some of the local artwork in his collection through the barter system. Before artist Maggie Russell asked David to sit for this portrait to display in a home show (and gave the painting to him afterward), he made her jewelry. "I made jewelry for her mom, and her mom baked me a zucchini bread," he says. Other pieces in the gallery wall are by Capt. James V, Mia Saine, and Booth Sartain McGee.*

LEFT: *"This is the embodiment of me in furniture," David says about the plush velvet armchair in a pattern inspired by West African wax print fabrics. He had already traced his ancestry back to England, France, Spain, and parts of the Caribbean, but it wasn't until he cross-referenced two DNA tests that he was able to track more than a quarter of his lineage to Nigeria. After learning that the cofounder of Albany Park, the maker of the chair, had discovered his own Nigerian ancestry the same way, David knew he needed this piece in his home. Besides reflecting his story, the chair also checks another top priority: "Honestly, I choose my furniture to be nappable." Soft velvet and a deep seat don't disappoint. "I go to sleep in these chairs—often!"*

When he returned to his house a year later, it felt like a second chance. "By the time I got back here, I was like, 'You have a whole house that you can love on, that you can decorate, you can redesign, you can bust down walls if you want to, build things—let's go for it!'" he says. "I'm going to do right by this house this time," he vowed.

True to his word, he refreshed the house in stages, beginning with the bedroom. He wanted the space to have depth, but he wasn't feeling the dismal gray paint the renters had left behind. "I knew I wanted to do at least one moody wall," he says, indicating the blue accent wall, painted Opera Glasses by Behr, "but I wanted the light to reflect a little bit better. I wanted it to wake me up," he explains the reasoning behind leaving the other walls white. Next, he redid the dining room, crowning the round table with an adjustable pendant light whose copper-toned glow captures the feeling of

ABOVE: *"Plumbing does not like me," David says, recalling the water that flowed onto the floor the day he replaced the kitchen faucet. By DIY-ing most of the home projects himself, he is able to substantially lower the cost of these upgrades—even if he has to learn along the way. Repainting cabinets is one of the most affordable ways to update a kitchen; follow David's lead and paint just the lower cabinets to get a fresh look for half the effort.*

OPPOSITE: *David brushed over the dreary gray paint with a royal blue accent wall.*

Rufus and Chaka Khan's song "Everlasting Love," David says.

When planning the kitchen updates, he balanced lofty goals with a $500 budget. "I wanted a big change, but I didn't want to spend that much," he says. "I just wanted enough to make me feel happy . . . I wanted it to feel like those dance parties that I now have in the kitchen." He perked up the drab taupe walls with fresh white paint, then brushed Sparkling Emerald by Behr on the lower cabinets. Flashes of gold—the faucet and cabinet hardware—reflect David's signature shade of yellow. "That's how I view life, mentally, that's where I am all the time. It's kind of like everything's yellow, everything's nice, and I want to translate that back into where I live." He plans to eventually revamp the room with a full-on renovation, complete with a new floor and backsplash, but for now, affordable upgrades like paint and metallic hardware help him feel at home.

Dedicating himself to home design the second time around has transformed David's perception of the house and the role it plays in his life. "I always say this isn't my forever home, but last year kind of changed that," he says. "It's my 'we'll talk about it' home." Investing in the house, along with finding his place in Memphis's burgeoning design community, has helped him envision living here long-term. "It's still very traditional, but Memphis is starting to break out and color is championed, not only in homes, but for people. Diversity is finally being championed." With many more projects on the horizon—he intends to turn the sunroom into a reception area for his growing roster of interior design clients—the house is inching closer and closer to a home he would have a hard time leaving. "I love it because it was built out of love," he says. "I don't believe in doing anything without a layer of love."

OPPOSITE: *Dark teal dining chairs pull an accent color from the hand-painted mural.*

embrace your space

Incorporating color into your decor has a powerful influence on the emotional register of your home. When choosing hues, and particularly when selecting paint, factors like light and layout are important, but the feeling each color evokes may be even more critical. Colors can reflect your personality, your cultural heritage, the landscape in which you were raised, and the landscape outside your door; they can create a home that's warm or cool, open or intimate. Identify the hues that feel like home to you and decorating with color will become more intuitive.

Pick a Palette

You may already know which colors speak to you—but if not, spending time with various hues might help. Looking to paint your home office? Brush a sample pot of paint on the wall in front of your desk or order a peel-and-stick paint sample, placing it wherever you can spot the color while you work. Over several days, note not only how the color looks but also how it affects your mood and your work. Did you feel focused, distracted, irritable? Try this method for any room you're looking to paint, observing how the color changes throughout the day in different light, as well as the mood it inspires. If you're feeling stuck, think about natural landscapes or environments where you feel most at home. It might be the rocky coastlines of Maine or the mossy forests of Washington or the sandy expanse of the California desert. Or invite in a hue borrowed from your travels—you won't be the first person to paint a door blue after a trip to Greece or a wall pink following a visit to Jaipur. Once you've found your personal color palette, determine

which of the colors work well together. Arrange paint chips, fabric swatches, and tile samples to see how they look in combination. Once you've made your selection, keep the paint chips or color swatches on hand so you can refer back to them as needed. Save them on your phone or a Pinterest board so you can match up colors when you're out at a store.

ABOVE: *Colors don't have to be loud to make a statement, as evidenced by the creamy white color palette found throughout Leanne's cabin.*

OPPOSITE: *Apprehensive about a big change? Take a tip from Matthew and Casey and paint just one wall at a time.*

Leave Negative Space

Just as in art, most rooms benefit from a bit of negative space and some room to breathe. In Matthew and Casey's apartment (pictured above), the white sofa set against a moody green wall gives the eye a spot to rest. The white rug interrupts the patterned parquet floor below. Color and pattern infuse a home with personality, but neutral colors like black and white offer some balance, a place to pause.

Start Small

For those who tend to stick to a neutral palette but want to explore more of the rainbow, consider painting a closet or bathroom first. A new hue will create a distinctive atmosphere in these little spaces—but if you get cold feet or want a refresh, it will require less time and money to repaint than a larger room. As you're working (and even once the project is complete), grant yourself the freedom to change your mind. When so many decisions in life have big consequences, giving yourself permission to rethink the small stuff can feel like such a gift.

Paint a Focal Point

Let one burst of color punctuate the space. If you don't have a headboard, try painting a colorful arch behind your bed. To delineate the work-from-home area on the side of your living room, paint a rectangle behind your desk. When you're ready for something new, painting over these areas will be even easier than repainting an accent wall.

Color Outside the Lines

If you're looking for some fresh paint ideas, forget the walls. Paint the ceiling in your bathroom like David's (pictured opposite), your kitchen cabinets like Lisa's (page 71) and David's (page 153), or the interior doors like Lisa's (page 71). Highlight architectural elements by lining an archway in a contrasting color or painting the trim a few shades darker than the walls. Or let paint create the illusion of architectural interest—paint just the lower third of each wall for a faux wainscoting effect.

Pick the Right Paint

To make your painting project healthier for you and the environment, stick to low- or no-VOC paints. VOCs (volatile organic compounds) are the chemicals released into the air as paint dries, and some paints can off-gas these chemicals for months. Fortunately, most major paint companies now offer lines of low- or zero-VOC paints. There are also some chemical-free alternatives to traditional paint. Limewash, for example, is made from lime putty (crushed limestone that's been burned and blended with water) that is mixed with natural pigments and thinned with more water. When brushed onto plaster walls or drywall that's been primed, it leaves a matte, textured effect with subtle movement. Milk paint is another historical stand-in for modern paint, crafted from milk protein (casein), lime, and natural pigments. It produces rich colors with a velvety finish. Especially if you'll be staying in your place while you paint, these options can spare you from breathing in harmful fumes.

OPPOSITE: *When plotting the design scheme for the bathroom, David's goal was to "make it feel like a party" the moment you open the door. Inspired by the artwork of Monica Lewis, he hand-painted a brushstroke pattern on the walls, then painted the ceiling with Dash of Curry by Behr. Gold fixtures invite glamour to the party.*

Repaint a Rental (with Permission)

Some property owners are fine with their tenants painting the walls, as long as they repaint them white before moving. Others won't ask you to repaint, since they were already planning to paint between tenants (and in some cities, they may even be legally required to do so). When I was searching for an apartment, I always asked what the policy was on painting. If I got a firm "No," I knew it wasn't the match for me—if they weren't keen on painting, they probably wouldn't go for any of my more involved home project ideas, either. Not sure where your building's property owner or management company stands on the big paint debate? Just ask. Don't worry: If it's a no-go, there's a wide array of reversible ways to decorate with color and pattern.

Curate an Art Gallery

This one's for you, renters and paint-shy homeowners: Rather than commit to color on the walls, think of your home as your own personal art gallery. White walls and neutral furniture provide a blank canvas for colorful artwork, wall hangings, ceramics, and decorative objects. Bonus: You won't have to repaint any walls when you move, and you can take all the color with you to your next place. Many of the walls in David's home are white, but the house overall feels vibrant, thanks to his collection of local artwork, colorful textiles, and abundant houseplants.

Turn to Textiles

Bedding, throw pillows, curtains, and blankets let you layer colors and patterns—without picking up a paintbrush or rolling on wallpaper. Considering just how much real estate a bed takes up in a bedroom, swapping out the duvet cover can change the design of the entire room. In the living room, the sofa is the star. If yours isn't in ideal condition or no longer reflects your style, textiles can help. Drape a blanket over the arm, pop on some throw pillows, or wrap the cushions in a colorful quilt to adorn the sofa with color (while concealing any stains at the same time).

OPPOSITE: *This vibrant painting, bought on the beach in the Dominican Republic, reflects David's love for music and dance.*

Stick-On Solutions

For those who are renting or want temporary fixes as they save up for a big reno, these removable products are stylish stopgaps.

Adhesive backsplash: Freshen up an outdated backsplash with stick-on subway tiles. Each adhesive-backed piece contains multiple tiles, and they fit together like a puzzle. Once you reach the edges of the backsplash, trim off excess using a craft knife.

Contact paper: Wrap your kitchen counter in marble self-adhesive vinyl film like Lisa did, (page 71) for a faux-stone look. If you have patience and are good with a craft knife, you'll be able to position the film around the sink and other obstacles. Once the film is in place, caulk around the sink so water won't seep underneath. You can also wrap kitchen cabinets in contact paper or cover the front of an appliance, like a refrigerator or dishwasher, to change the color.

Electrical tape and washi tape: Line window panes with electrical tape, or use extra-wide washi tape to update flat-front cabinets.

Magnetic appliance covers: Wish you had a stainless-steel refrigerator? Give old fridges or dishwashers a makeover with magnetic, custom-cut covers in sleek stainless steel or playful patterns.

Peel-and-stick wallpaper: Designed to cover smooth surfaces, temporary wallpaper is like a giant sticker for your walls. Slowly peel the backing off the wallpaper roll and adhere it to the wall, starting at the top and working your way down in small sections (see Fiona's kitchen wall, page 40). As you go, use your hands or a straightedge (a credit card or squeegee works) to smooth out air bubbles. No DIY experience necessary—just take your time removing air bubbles and lining up each strip of wallpaper. When you're ready for a change, slowly unpeel the paper.

Tile decals: Change the color or design of the tiles in your home by smoothing floor decals over the top, like Natasha did in her kitchen (page 62).

Note: *Even adhesive products that are designed to be removable can leave sticky residue behind if they get too hot or are left on too long. Store-bought adhesive remover can help—just test it in an inconspicuous spot first.*

OPPOSITE: *Let accessories lend color to your space, as Natasha did with the blue and green ceramics and glassware dotting her kitchen shelves.*

AFTERWORD

E ven before you debate paint chips or peruse peel-and-stick wallpapers, the decision
to embrace your space starts with a shift in mentality. It's a choice to invest—whether
time, money, or creative energy—in your home. For some, that means a floor-to-
ceiling makeover. For others, it's a decluttered closet or an organized drawer. Regardless of
how big or small of a material change this book prompts you to make, I hope it will change
how you think about your home. You can love where you live, even if you rent. You can create
a home that makes you happy, even if you plan to move in a few years. You can decorate a
space that feels like you, no matter your budget.

You don't have to do it all at once, and you don't even have to finish the project before you
move out. The renters and homeowners featured have all followed their own timelines. Lisa
(page 69) spent eight years in her studio before she decided to make it her own, whereas
when Julia and her roommates (page 85) moved into their loft, the cardboard boxes were
gone by day one and the place was fully decorated within two weeks. Go ahead, declutter and
decorate at your own pace, but make the decision to embrace your space starting right now.

To jump-start the process, try a ten-minute decluttering challenge (page 29) or make over
your living room in an afternoon (page 81). Refresh your kitchen without remodeling: Follow
David's lead and replace the cabinet hardware (page 153), then take a cue from Natasha and
revamp the floor with vinyl stick-on tiles (page 62). Slow down to select furniture pieces
you'll want to live with long-term, and you'll happily haul them to your next place. Put down
roots by potting a plant or sprinkling some seeds. As Kaylyn has discovered, the journey of
a gardener requires patience. Consider potted plants you can take with you when you move
(page 125), or leave a gift to those who will live there after you by planting perennials that
will come back year after year.

I believe there's power in embracing your space—and that this decision can transform your
life. Repaint your home office and observe how it changes your feelings about work. String
up some lights, set up a picnic table, and watch how quickly your patio becomes a gathering
spot for friends. Reorganize your kitchen and notice how much more you enjoy cooking dinner
at home. Thoughtful design isn't just about creating beautiful spaces (although it's certainly
a bonus!), but it's also about crafting a space that supports your life. Thoughtful design is
about maximizing the square footage you have. It's about making the most of where you
are right now. And it's for everyone.

FOLLOW ALONG

Check out the social media accounts, websites, and businesses of the featured renters and homeowners.

KELLY BROWN AND BRYCE EHRECKE
(page 11)
Kelly Brown Photographer
KellyBrownPhotographer.com
Instagram: @kellybrownphoto

CRÉ NATURAL BUILDING
CreNaturalBuilding.com
Instagram: @crenaturalbuilding

LEANNE FORD AND ERIK ALLEN FORD
(page 19)
Leanne Ford Interiors
LeanneFord.com
Instagram: @leannefordinteriors

BUCK MASON
BuckMason.com
Instagram: @buckmason

FIONA BYRNE
(page 35)
NycFiona.com
Instagram: @nycfiona

KATE HAMILTON GRAY
(page 45)
Hamilton Gray Studio
HamiltonGray.studio
Instagram: @hamiltongraystudio

NATASHA NYANIN
(page 61)
NatashaNyanin.com
Instagram: @natashanyanin

LISA LU
(page 69)
Instagram: @hello_lulu
@casa__lulu

JULIA STEVENS
(page 85)
Instagram: @juliastevens_

PARIS FABRIKANT
(page 85)
Instagram: @parisfab

TORI JENNER
(page 85)
Instagram: @victoriabennettjenner

LINDSAY MACRAE
(page 93)
Lindsay MacRae Interiors
LindsayMacRae.com
Instagram: @lindsaymacraeinteriors

AYA MACEDA AND KURT ARNOLD
(page 113)
ALAO Design
ALAO.design
Instagram: @alao_design

VISUAL CAPTIVITY
VisualCaptivity.com
Instagram: @visualcaptivity

KAYLYN HEWITT
(page 123)
True Vine Studio
TrueVineStudios.com
Instagram: @truevinestudio

MATTHEW DEROSIER
(page 139)
Instagram: @brooklynartboy

DAVID QUARLES IV
(page 147)
DavidQuarlesIV.com
Instagram: @david.quarlesiv

IVBYDAVID.COM
Instagram: @ivbydavid

embrace your space

166

STYLING CREDITS

ADRIAN MANUEL
A Stylish Sanctuary (page 69)
AdrianTManuel.com
Instagram: @adriantmanuel

HILARY ROBERTSON
Cabin Crush (page 19)
HilaryRobertson.com
Instagram: @hilaryrobertson

MARIANA MARCKI-MATOS
Studio of Splendors (page 61);
An Old-World Abode (page 139)
MarianaMarckiMatos.com
Instagram: @marianamarcki

embrace your space

FURTHER READING

IF YOU WANT MORE SPACE-SAVING IDEAS . . .

Apartment Therapy's Big Book of Small, Cool Spaces by Maxwell Ryan
  (Potter Style)

*Small Space Style: Because You Don't Need to Live Large to Live
  Beautifully* by Whitney Leigh Morris (Weldon Owen)

The Little Book of Living Small by Laura Fenton (Gibbs Smith)

IF YOU WANT MORE RENTAL HACKS . . .

*Rental Style: The Ultimate Guide to Decorating Your Apartment or
  Small Home* by Chelsey Brown (Skyhorse)

IF YOU'RE NOT DONE DECLUTTERING . . .

*Minimalista: Your Step-by-Step Guide to a Better Home, Wardrobe, and
  Life* by Shira Gill (Ten Speed Press)

The Afrominimalist's Guide to Living with Less by Christine Platt (S&S/
  Simon Element)

IF YOU WANT MORE HELP GETTING ORGANIZED . . .

Beautifully Organized: A Guide to Function and Style in Your Home
  by Nikki Boyd (Paige Tate & Co.)

*Remodelista: The Organized Home: Simple, Stylish Storage Ideas for All
  Over the House* by Julie Carlson and Margot Guralnick (Artisan)

*The Real Simple Method to Organizing Every Room: And How to Keep It
  That Way* by the Editors of *Real Simple* (TI Inc. Books)

IF YOU WANT MORE MINIMALIST DECOR IDEAS . . .

Monochrome Home: Elegant Interiors in Black and White
  by Hilary Robertson (Ryland Peters & Small)

IF YOU WANT MORE COLORFUL DECOR IDEAS . . .

Living with Color: Inspiration and How-Tos to Brighten Up Your Home
  by Rebecca Atwood (Clarkson Potter)

IF YOU WANT MORE PLANT INSPIRATION . . .

Wild at Home: How to Style and Care for Beautiful Plants
  by Hilton Carter (CICO Books)

SHOPPING SOURCES

PREOWNED AND VINTAGE

CHAIRISH (Chairish.com): Online marketplace for vintage and antique pieces, including high-end designer furniture.

CRAIGSLIST (Craigslist.org): Preowned furniture and antiques for local pickup.

FACEBOOK MARKETPLACE (Facebook.com): Large selection of vintage and preowned furniture and decor for pickup or delivery.

SIDEWALK FINDS: If you live in a city, keep an eye out for furniture, lamps, and appliances left out for free on the sidewalk. Avoid pieces with upholstery, and clean everything thoroughly before bringing it inside.

MARKETS

Search your local flea market for pieces with history, or plan a trip to one of these famous antiques fairs—they're worth the journey.

BRIMFIELD ANTIQUES FLEA MARKET *BRIMFIELD, MA* **(BrimfieldAntiqueFleaMarket.com):** A triannual flea market full of vintage treasures and collectibles held in the spring, summer, and fall.

ROSE BOWL FLEA MARKET *PASADENA, CA* **(RGCShows.com):** On the second Sunday of every month, thousands of vendors gather at the Rose Bowl Stadium to sell antiques and local art.

ROUND TOP ANTIQUES SHOW *ROUND TOP, TX* **(RoundTopTexasAntiques.com):** A sprawling, twenty-mile-long antiques fair held in the spring and fall.

FURNITURE

ARTICLE (Article.com): Sectionals that can fit in a studio? Find them here.

IKEA (Ikea.com): Affordable Scandinavian style that stands the test of time (some best sellers, like the Billy bookcase, have been sold for decades) and can be hacked using paint, new hardware, and more for a custom look. For Ikea hacks, try **Semihandmade (Semihandmade.com)** for fronts for cabinets; **Norse Interiors (NorseInteriors.com)** for cabinet doors and furniture legs; **Bemz (Bemz.com)** for sofa covers; **Comfort Works (Comfort-Works.com)** for sofa covers; and **Prettypegs (Prettypegs.com)** for furniture legs.

RESTORATION HARDWARE (RH.com): Shop the kid and teen sections for RH's signature elevated style at slightly lower price points.

URBAN OUTFITTERS (UrbanOutfitters.com): For fresh trend-driven furniture and clever storage for tight spaces.

WEST ELM (WestElm.com): Check out its small-space section for multitasking pieces with built-in storage.

FURNITURE TO RENT

If you're only going to be in a city for a few months, consider renting your furniture. That way, you won't have to invest in pieces you know you'll soon sell (or worse, send to the landfill).

FEATHER (LiveFeather.com): Rent furniture from brands like Floyd and West Elm, with the option to buy any pieces you like. Available in select cities.

FERNISH (Fernish.com): Stylish selection of furniture and decor to rent, with free pickup at the end of your lease. Currently available in Austin, Dallas, New York City, Seattle, Washington, D.C., and parts of Southern California.

DECOR

ANTHROPOLOGIE (Anthropologie.com): Go-to spot for pieces with personality, from ornate mirrors to patterned lampshades.

ETSY (Etsy.com): Vintage and handmade pieces from thousands of vendors around the world.

H&M HOME (HM.com): On-trend art, vases, and baskets, plus inexpensive linen bedding.

JAMALI GARDEN (JamaliGarden.com): A favorite source among event planners and magazine editors, and stocked with mercury glass vases, candleholders, ceramic planters, and holiday decor.

JUNGALOW (Jungalow.com): Color and texture abound in this online shop offering throw pillows, art prints, patterned wallpaper, and more.

WORLD MARKET (WorldMarket.com): An eclectic mix of rugs, lamps, mirrors, and woven baskets.

ZARA HOME (ZaraHome.com): Sophisticated, European-inspired style at reasonable prices.

ORGANIZERS

CONTAINER STORE (ContainerStore.com): The ultimate source for all things organization, from clothes hangers and clear shoeboxes to wall hooks and custom closets.

MUJI (Muji.us): Streamlined storage for jewelry, accessories, and office supplies.

OPEN SPACES (GetOpenSpaces.com): Clean lines and fun colors combine forces in minimalist entryway racks, storage bins, and acrylic containers.

YAMAZAKI HOME (TheYamazakiHome.com): Well-designed storage for tight spaces, including slim rolling carts for the kitchen and magnetic organization racks for the side of the fridge.

PLANT SUPPLIES

TERRAIN (ShopTerrain.com): Pots and plant stands for indoor jungles, gardening tools and string lights for outdoor spaces.

REMOVABLE ADHESIVE PRODUCTS

CONTACT PAPER: The Home Depot (HomeDepot.com), Lowe's (Lowes.com), Target (Target.com).

MAGNETIC APPLIANCE COVERS: Appliance Art (EasyHomeRenewals.com), Etsy (Etsy.com).

PEEL-AND-STICK WALLPAPER AND DECALS: Chasing Paper (ChasingPaper.com), Hygge & West (HyggeAndWest.com), Tempaper (Tempaper.com), Spoonflower (Spoonflower.com), Urban Outfitters (UrbanOutfitters.com), Etsy (Etsy.com), Walls Need Love (WallsNeedLove.com), Urbanwalls (UwDecals.com).

STICK-ON BACKSPLASH: WallPops (WallPops.com), The Home Depot (HomeDepot.com).

TILE DECALS: Etsy (Etsy.com), Mirth Studio (MirthStudio.com), Quadrostyle (Quadrostyle.com).

ACKNOWLEDGMENTS

When I was a kid, I believed that if I could just harness the wherewithal to stay up all night, I could write a book. In reality, I wasn't far off. Writing this book while keeping my beloved day job at *Real Simple* was the result of one late night after another, after another, after another. Thanks to Chris for keeping the bed warm while I burned the midnight oil. (And for all the edits.) I love you. And to my "feral"-turned-lap-cat, Beef, for keeping me company on the couch.

Thank you to my parents, who modeled tenacity and creativity in equal measure, and taught me what it means to build a home and life you love. You're right: Life is better by the lake.

Thank you to Kelsey, for being tough yet fair. Your honesty and good eye were more valuable than you know. Thanks to Brian, for blazing your own trail so that others could do the same.

Thank you to my extended family on both sides for your support and for asking interesting questions so that this book could offer better answers.

Thank you to all my art club/studio art friends, who are much more talented and chill than me for fielding my anxiety-ridden texts and phone calls. You are true besties.

Thanks to all the teachers and mentors who have guided me over the years: Your imagined edits were rattling around in my head the entire time. Thank you to Diana Kuan at the Brooklyn Brainery for teaching me everything I know about book proposals. And special thanks to Laura Fenton for the invaluable advice and guidance on the book-writing process.

Thank you to Katie Killebrew, for finding my words scribbled across the internet and believing I could do this. Thank you to John Foster for so expertly shepherding this project, and to the Weldon Owen art team for bringing this book to life.

Thank you to Genevieve—I couldn't imagine a better copilot on this ride. Thanks for saying yes to a stranger, hopping on planes, renting cars, trekking through the desert (without coffee, no less), working your soft-styling magic, and making this book a visual wonderland that I'm so happy to get lost in.

Big thanks to Brittany Barb for photo assisting and for the laughs, and to Quinn Sherman for all the photo retouching work. Thanks to Noel Knostman and Anthony Hardge for coordinating.

To the stylists who helped these homes shine even brighter—Hilary Robertson, Mariana Marcki-Matos, and Adrian Manuel—thank you. With thanks to Amy Neunsinger for hand-delivering beautiful emergency props at a moment's notice.

To the renters and homeowners featured within these pages, you are the heart and soul of this book. Thank you for opening your doors and sharing your stories.

INDEX

weldonowen

an imprint of Insight Editions
P.O. Box 3088
San Rafael, CA 94912
www.weldonowen.com

CEO Raoul Goff
VP Publisher Roger Shaw
Editorial Director Katie Killebrew
Senior Editor John Foster
VP Creative Chrissy Kwasnik
Art Director Allister Fein
VP Manufacturing Alix Nicholaeff
Production Manager Joshua Smith
Sr Production Manager, Subsidiary Rights
Lina s Palma-Temena

Weldon Owen would like to thank Jessica Easto for copyediting, Karen Levy for proofreading, Timothy Griffin for indexing, and Matt Killebrew for design.

ISBN: 978-1-68188-851-4

Manufactured in China by Insight Editions
10 9 8 7 6 5 4 3 2 1

ABOUT THE AUTHOR + PHOTOGRAPHER

KATIE HOLDEFEHR is a writer who loves home decor that's handmade and nature-made. She is currently the associate editorial director at *Real Simple* and has previously worked at *Apartment Therapy*, *Martha Stewart Living*, and *Good Housekeeping*. When she's not writing, you'll find her installing wainscoting and painting cabinets in her ninety-year-old Brooklyn apartment.

KatieHoldefehr.com
Instagram: @katieholdefehr

GENEVIEVE GARRUPPO is just as passionate about design as she is about photography. She has contributed to *Architectural Digest*, *Elle Decor*, *Galerie*, and *New York* magazine, among many others. She currently resides in Brooklyn.

GenevieveGarruppo.com
Instagram: @garruppo

ROOTS of PEACE   REPLANTED PAPER

Insight Editions, in association with Roots of Peace, will plant two trees for each tree used in the manufacturing of this book. Roots of Peace is an internationally renowned humanitarian organization dedicated to eradicating land mines worldwide and converting war-torn lands into productive farms and wildlife habitats. Roots of Peace will plant two million fruit and nut trees in Afghanistan and provide farmers there with the skills and support necessary for sustainable land use.